Asian Economic Trends and Their Security Implications

Charles Wolf, Jr.

Anil Bamezai

K. C. Yeh

Benjamin Zycher

Prepared for the
Office of the Secretary of Defense/United States Army

National Defense Research Institute/Arroyo Center

RAND

This report is the final product of a project dealing with the security implications of Asia's financial and economic turmoil. After considering the sharp economic reversals suffered in the Asian region in 1997 and 1998, and the marked but widely varying evidence of significant recovery among the different countries of the region, the report considers the medium- and longer-term trends with respect to economic growth, military spending, and military investment in five countries in the greater Asian area: Japan, China, India, South Korea, and Indonesia. The five countries included in this study were selected by agreement with the sponsors from a larger set addressed in RAND's previous analyses in 1989 and 1995 of long-term economic and military trends. India, a South Asian country, was included along with the four principal East Asian countries in light of its size and enhanced military prominence.

Following the analysis of these longer-term economic and military trends, the report considers the security implications of these trends with respect to alternative security environments in the region, changes in the intraregional balance of military and economic power, and such other issues as prospects for multilateral security cooperation, support for forward-based U.S. forces in the region, and alliance burden sharing.

This research was sponsored by the Office of Net Assessment in the Department of Defense and the Office of the Deputy Chief of Staff for Intelligence in the U.S. Army. The project was executed jointly through RAND's National Defense Research Institute (NDRI) and the Strategy, Doctrine, and Resources Program of RAND's Arroyo Center.

NDRI and the Arroyo Center are both federally funded research and development centers, the former sponsored by the Office of the Secretary of Defense, the Joint Staff, the unified commands, and the defense agencies, and the latter by the United States Army.

The report should be of interest and use to those in the policy community who are concerned with strategic and contingency planning, and impending changes in the balance of forces among the major countries in the region.

CONTENTS

FIGURES

TABLES

SUMMARY

In 1995, RAND issued a report on long-term economic and military trends in Asia, covering the period from 1994 to 2015.[1] The principal aim of the present report is to review, revise, and update our previous estimates in light of the new economic conditions prevailing in the region, and to draw appropriate inferences from the new estimates with respect to security issues in the region. The earlier report mainly used data from the 1980s and early 1990s, which were periods of high and sustained growth throughout Asia. In Japan, annual economic growth in the 1980s was about 4 percent. China's growth was estimated at nearly double-digit annual rates. India's growth was almost 5 percent per year. High as well as dramatically rising annual rates of gross domestic product (GDP) growth were experienced by the rest of East Asia (including both the initial set of "tigers": South Korea, Taiwan, Hong Kong, and Singapore; and the second cohort of aspiring tigers in Southeast Asia: Indonesia, Thailand, and Malaysia). (All future references to "Korea" are to "South Korea," except where otherwise noted in the text.)

---

[1]See Charles Wolf, Jr., K. C. Yeh, Anil Bamezai, Donald P. Henry, and Michael Kennedy, *Long-Term Economic and Military Trends 1994–2015: The United States and Asia*, Santa Monica, Calif.: RAND, MR-627-OSD, 1995; see also unpublished RAND research by Charles Wolf, Jr. and Michael Kennedy on long-term economic and military trends in Russia, Germany, and Indonesia. These 1995 documents followed earlier work on the same general subject produced for the National Commission on Integrated Long-Term Strategy in 1988 and 1989, and reported in Charles Wolf, Jr., K. C. Yeh, Anil Bamezai, Benjamin Zycher, et al., *Long-Term Economic and Military Trends, 1950–2010*, Santa Monica, Calif.: RAND, N-2757-USDP, 1989.

In July of 1997, Asia experienced sharp economic reversals that have been variously described as a financial "meltdown," a spreading economic "contagion," or simply as serious economic turmoil.

Following the collapse of the Thai baht in July 1997, asset values in the four Asian "crisis" countries—Thailand, Korea, Indonesia, and Malaysia—plummeted by about 75 percent as a result of the combined effects of currency depreciation and deflated property and equity markets. Economic growth in the four countries fell to substantial negative rates.

This report begins by briefly considering previous RAND forecasts for Asia and the sharp economic reversals experienced in the region in 1997 and 1998.

We then consider in more detail Asia's economic turmoil triggered by the collapse of the Thai baht in mid-1997. We examine the varied record of recovery from that turmoil achieved by the "crisis" countries—Korea, Thailand, Malaysia, and Indonesia. We also consider the quite different circumstances and economic problems of Japan and China, both of which have been only modestly affected by the sharp economic reversals in the crisis countries, although each is afflicted with serious economic problems predating and transcending those reversals. This assessment is based on data up to and including September 1999.

With this as background, we summarize the forecasting model we have used and present new estimates for GDP, per-capita GDP, military spending, and military capital in Japan, China, India, Korea, and Indonesia. In all cases, we present results for each of the four key variables in terms of both "nominal" exchange rates (XR), and "real" purchasing-power-parity (PPP) rates. For military capital, the purchasing-power equivalent used in making conversions from constant-price local currencies to U.S. dollars is a purchasing-power-parity measure applying to investment goods (PI), rather than to the GDP of each country as a whole. We explain the differing concepts, purposes, and relevance underlying the use of nominal and real exchange rates, respectively.

Furthermore, we identify and explain instances in which there are significant differences between our current estimates and those made in previous RAND studies in 1995 and 1989 of long-term economic and military trends.

The estimates presented in this report are intended as reasonable forecasts based on explicit assumptions about certain key parameters as explained fully in the text and in Appendix B. This does not preclude other reasonable forecasts, nor does it imply that the ones presented here are the most likely ones.

Among the major points of the new trend estimates are the following (all of the dollar figures are in 1998 U.S. dollars converted from constant-price national currency values):

JAPAN

- The estimated GDP growth rate varies from 1 percent to 1.6 percent per annum over the period from 2000 to 2015.

- Between 2000 and 2015, per-capita GDP rises from about $44 thousand to about $54 thousand in XR terms, or from about $23 thousand to $29 thousand in PPP terms.

- For military spending, the estimate for 2000 is approximately $61 billion, rising to $75 billion in 2015 in XR terms, and from $33 billion in 2000 to $40 billion in 2015 in PPP terms.

- Japan's military capital stock increases from about $112 billion in 2000 to $119 billion in 2015 in PI terms, and from $154 billion to $166 billion in XR terms, based on annual military investment in the 15-year period, and depreciation of previously accumulated military capital.

CHINA

Two scenarios are used in making the forecasts for China: Scenario A is the sustained growth scenario, and Scenario B is a disrupted growth scenario.

- In Scenario A, China's GDP approximately doubles by 2015; it increases by only 50 percent in Scenario B.

- The growth rate for Scenario A over the period is slightly above 5 percent annually, while in Scenario B the corresponding growth rate is below 3 percent.

- By 2015, China's GDP in Scenario A is more than 3 times that of Japan in PPP terms, but only 36 percent of Japan's if nominal exchange rates are used for the conversions. In Scenario B, the China GDP forecasts are more than 30 percent below those in Scenario A. Scenario B reduces China's relative GDP estimates by about one-third.

- China's per-capita GDP doubles between 2000 and 2015, but still remains below $10 thousand in 2015, in the favorable Scenario A.

- China's military spending and military capital rise substantially in Scenario A, as a consequence of forecasted GDP growth and military investment, respectively. By 2015, in Scenario A, China's military capital is more than 4 times that of Japan in terms of the PPP value of the yuan for investment goods (PI), and about the same as Japan's military capital in terms of nominal exchange rates.

- In Scenario B, China's military spending and military capital are, respectively, 45 percent and 30 percent below those in Scenario A. China's Scenario B would reduce the estimates for China by about one-third, relative to those of Japan.

INDIA

- India's GDP more than doubles between 2000 and 2015, reaching about 54 percent of China's GDP—about 5 percent greater than its present GDP relative to China's.

- Per-capita GDP reaches $5.1 thousand, about 60 percent of China's.

- Military spending increases more than two-and-one-half times from the present level by 2015.

- By 2015, India's military capital reaches $314 billion, which is about 62 percent of China's ($666 billion), compared with only 48 percent of China's military capital in 2000.

KOREA

- GDP and per-capita GDP more than double between 2000 and 2015. Korea's GDP rises during this 15-year period, from about one-quarter of Japan's GDP to nearly one-half by 2015 (in PPP dollars).

- Military spending increases substantially, from $25 billion in 1998 PPP dollars in 2000 to $54 billion in 2015.

- Military capital increases by 85 percent from 2000 to 2015, from $61 billion to $114 billion in 2015. Thus, by 2015, Korea's military capital would be approximately equal to that of Japan, whereas Korea's current military capital is less than 60 percent of Japan's.

INDONESIA

- GDP will probably regain its 1995 level by 2005.

- Military spending in PPP terms will be about half that of Korea.

- Although Indonesia's military capital rises sharply over the period from 2000 to 2015, it falls appreciably relative to the military capital stock of the other four countries.

We also consider the question of how to link the separate country forecasts, and we propose two methods: (1) regional indexing and (2) formulating alternative security environments for the Asian region.

The first method uses the respective GDPs of the five countries and their military capital stocks as rough proxy indicators of relative economic and military power, respectively. While acknowledging that each of these indicators is only partial and suggestive rather than definitive, their use contributes to an assessment of changes in the balance of forces in the region. These two indicators are indexed for the five countries, using Korea's GDP and military capital in 2000 as the base and expressing the other four countries' indexes in relation to this base. Several significant points emerge from these indexes:

- Japan's relative economic and military power in the region diminishes appreciably from 2000 to 2015, vis-à-vis those of both China and Korea.

- As a consequence, the value that Japan will place on its security alliance with the United States is likely to rise, and/or Japanese efforts to reform and liberalize its economy and to enhance its military capabilities may also grow.

- China's economic and military power does not rise relative to that of Korea's, and diminishes somewhat relative to India's. However, the absolute gap between China's GDP and military capital, on the one hand, and those of the other principal countries, on the other, grows substantially.

- Indonesia's relative and absolute stature in the region recedes.

For the second approach to the question of how to link the forecasts, we formulate two sharply different scenarios to bracket a wide range of future possibilities. These contrasting alternatives use as building blocks aspects of our forecasts for the five countries, while introducing other considerations not addressed in these forecasts, such as conjectures about the status of alliance relationships in the region, as well as possible regional conflicts. The two bracketing scenarios are Scenario A, which we term "Chinese Preponderance," and Scenario B, characterized as "Sustained Intraregional Balance."

In Scenario A, China sustains a high annual GDP growth rate, and its aggregate military share of its growing GDP moves toward the higher end of the 2–3 percent range used in our forecasts. However, Japan, Korea, and other countries in the region maintain low defense shares of their slower-growing economies, and India's economic growth and defense modernization progress slowly. Also in this scenario, we consider that U.S. alliances with Japan and Korea are attenuated, and forward-based U.S. forces are reduced. Under these circumstances, it is not implausible that the preponderance of Chinese power in the region might be asserted by enforcing its national claims in the Paracels, the Spratlys, and Taiwan.

In Scenario B, China's growth slows to that reflected in our past "disrupted-growth" forecasts, and its military spending and military modernization progress slowly. Japan resumes appreciable economic growth within two or three years and maintains or raises its defense spending as a share of GDP. Also, Japan's military modernization is further enhanced by growing concerns about the unpredictable behavior of North Korea's long-range missile testing. South Korea resumes substantial economic growth and maintains its defense spending and military investment because of continued uncertainty about the North Korean threat. At the same time, India's economic growth and defense modernization progress significantly, and U.S. alliances and forward-based forces are sustained.

The resulting balance of forces implied by Scenario B, including an implicit assumption that Taiwan's own military and its economic capabilities are maintained, would provide a constraining security environment, although not one that would assure regional stability.

In our final analysis, we address several questions raised at the inception of this study by U.S. Army planners and decisionmakers. These questions and our abbreviated responses to them are summarized below:

- Will Asia's economic problems make the region more bellicose or more peaceful? We suggest that a middle position is more likely—namely, attitudes of "caution" and "restraint" are likely to prevail—rather than either bellicosity or amity in the region.

- Will prospects for multilateral security cooperation in the region be encouraged or set back? We believe that the economic problems experienced in the Asian region are likely to impede rather than encourage efforts toward multilateral security cooperation in the Asia-Pacific region.

- How will and should alliance burden-sharing agreements related to forward-based U.S. forces be affected in Korea and Japan? We distinguish between the two countries: In Japan there may be a political argument, but there is not an economic one, for some reduction in burden sharing; in Korea, there is both an economic and political argument for such an adjustment.

- Will Asia's economic problems undermine or support the U.S. Army's presence in the region in general, and in Korea in particular? We suggest that, while the situations in Korea and Japan differ, endorsement and support of U.S. forward-based forces are

likely to remain strong in both countries. In Korea, this support
might be significantly reduced if and when unification between
North and South is achieved.

Chapter One

UPDATING AND IMPROVING PREVIOUS ESTIMATES IN LIGHT OF CHANGED CONDITIONS

Two familiar quotations are worth citing to clarify the objectives of this analysis. The first is President Eisenhower's truistic observation that "the future lies before us"; the second has been variously attributed to Mark Twain and Yogi Berra: "It is dangerous to make forecasts, especially about the future."

The period through 2015 remains "before us," as it was at the time of RAND's previous forecasting work in 1988–1989 and 1994–1995; and, as before, it remains hazardous to make forecasts.[1]

Nevertheless, the aim of this analysis is to update and improve upon our previous forecasts of economic and military trends in five countries (Japan, China, India, South Korea, and Indonesia), with respect to four indicators of their relative power and leverage, namely, gross domestic product (GDP), per-capita gross domestic product, military spending, and military capital (the latter representing the net accumulation of annual weapons procurement and military construction). We will also highlight and explain those instances where the

---

[1]See Charles Wolf, Jr., K. C. Yeh, Anil Bamezai, Donald P. Henry, and Michael Kennedy, *Long-Term Economic and Military Trends 1994–2015: The United States and Asia,* Santa Monica, Calif.: RAND, MR-627-OSD, 1995; see also unpublished RAND research by Charles Wolf, Jr. and Michael Kennedy on long-term economic and military trends in Russia, Germany, and Indonesia. These 1995 documents followed earlier work on the same general subject produced for the National Commission on Integrated Long-Term Strategy in 1988 and 1989, and reported in Charles Wolf, Jr., K. C. Yeh, Anil Bamezai, Benjamin Zycher, et al., *Long-Term Economic and Military Trends, 1950–2010,* Santa Monica, Calif.: RAND, N-2757-USDP, 1989.

present forecasts differ from our previous ones. Our focus on these five countries is explained by both their size and prominence, and by the interests of the sponsors of this research. In particular, India's inclusion reflects these considerations, as well as its heightened recent and prospective influence in the Asian region. Our present assessment is based on data up to and including September 1999.

We also employ these new forecasts to address several security-related issues, including the broad outlook for the Asian region's future security environment; the intraregional balance of forces; prospects for multilateral security cooperation and multilateral institutions; and prospective attitudes toward, and host country support for, U.S. forward-based forces in the region, notably in South Korea and Japan.

To facilitate comparisons between the current and previous estimates, we employ the same forecasting model used in the earlier study (see Appendix A).

The estimates presented in this report are intended as reasonable forecasts based on explicit assumptions about certain key parameters as explained fully in the text and in Appendix B. This does not preclude other reasonable forecasts, nor does it imply that the ones presented here are the most likely ones.

Our present forecasts differ from those made in 1994–1995 for several reasons:

- The use of more recent and better data, described in the individual country sections of Chapter Four.

- The sharp and unforeseen economic reversals and financial turmoil that occurred in East Asia in 1997 and 1998, as well as the remarkable recovery experienced by some of the East Asian countries since then.

- The use of both "nominal" exchange rates and "real" purchasing-power-parity rates for the dollar conversions from local currencies; the previous RAND work reported only purchasing-power-parity conversions.

- The present forecasts use purchasing-power-parity rates based on the latest (1995) Penn World Tables (PWT), rather than the 1989 PWT data employed in the earlier study.

Probably the largest differences from the earlier work arise in our estimates for Korea, reflecting sharp changes in the underlying assumptions. In 1994, following the death of Kim Il Sung, it was consensually anticipated that the anachronistic polity in North Korea would self-destruct through one or another scenario. In our earlier forecasts, we therefore postulated reunification by 1996 through one of three different scenarios: a "soft landing;" an East German–West German type of consolidation; or a military conflict through which North Korea would be defeated and would merge with South Korea. The resulting forecasts for Korea assumed a reunited South and North Korea which, after an initial setback lasting several years, would return to South Korea's prior high-growth path.[2] These assumptions and the forecasts based upon them were plainly wrong.

In our current estimates, we confine the forecasts to South Korea, positing that North Korea will maintain its separate status, without imposing appreciable extra economic burdens on the South, while South Korea itself will continue to recover smartly from the economic and financial turmoil of 1997–1998. (All future references to "Korea" are to "South Korea," except where otherwise noted in the text.) It is not inconceivable that these assumptions may also turn out to err.

As in the prior RAND studies, the present forecasts are made on a country-by-country basis; interactions among the countries are not allowed for in the estimating model, nor does the model directly allow for the effects of possible changes in international trade and capital flows. So, for example, we do not consider the extent to which Japan's and China's large current account surpluses are sustainable. In the concluding chapters, we briefly consider several potential interactive effects: for example, the possible effects on Japan of China's increased economic and military power, the possible effects on China of India's increased economic and military power,

---

[2]See Wolf et al., 1995, pp. 45–48.

and the potential effects on multilateral security cooperation in the Asian region resulting from the economic crisis of 1997–1998.

Chapter Two provides a brief review of the 1997–1998 Asian economic turmoil, and the marked progress in recovering from it in some parts of East Asia to a much greater extent than in others.

Chapter Three summarizes the principal results of our forecasts for each of the four indicators of economic and military trends that we have used—GDP, per-capita GDP, military spending, and military capital stock—in the five principal countries, Japan, China, India, Korea, and Indonesia, of the Asian region for the 2000–2015 time period.

Chapter Four presents detailed country-by-country forecasts, together with a brief account of the individual data sources and key parameters used for each of the five countries in applying the macroeconomic model described in Appendix A. The historical pattern of these parameters and reasons for the values assumed for them in this study are set forth in Appendix B. Also, limited sensitivity testing of these parameters and the results from it are summarized in Appendix B.

Chapter Five applies two approaches to aggregating the separate country estimates: (1) indexing the GDPs and military capital stocks of the five countries to show changes in the intraregional balance of power with respect to these metrics, together with a qualitative consideration of potential interaction effects on the individual country estimates; and (2) formulating two contrasting scenarios for the future security environments of the region by combining our forecasts with other possible developments in East Asia.

Finally, Chapter Six considers relations between our forecasts and several specific issues: (1) prevalence of bellicosity or amity in the region; (2) prospects for multilateral security cooperation; (3) burden sharing; and (4) attitudes toward U.S. Army presence in the region, especially in Korea.

Chapter Two

ASIA'S ECONOMIC TURMOIL AND THE VARIED RECORD OF RECOVERY

THE "CRISIS" COUNTRIES: KOREA, THAILAND, MALAYSIA, AND INDONESIA

The East Asian economic crisis, triggered by the collapse of the Thai baht in July 1997, is essentially over, as is the generalized fear of more severe global financial repercussions from it. Postmortem controversy continues in financial and academic circles over the extent to which the original crisis was due to the operation of "free" global markets, or instead to distortions created in these markets by mistaken policies and the lack of legal and financial institutions to redress them. Those who advocate the former of these two positions place primary responsibility for the original crisis on such phenomena as the sometimes "irrational exuberance" of markets and their susceptibility to "overshooting," and to the malady of "contagion." Those who identify with the second position—that bad policies rather than free markets are to blame—place primary emphasis on excessive short-term lending, pegged exchange rates, and the "moral hazards" created by a tacit belief that governments or multilateral agencies will provide a safety net if circumstances sour. This controversy is not likely to be resolved in the near future.

In any event, the earlier sense of economic crisis has been replaced by a situation characterized by widely differing economic performance among the East Asian countries and correspondingly differing problems and prospects. A brief overview of this situation requires distinguishing between four quite different sets of countries and economic circumstances: namely, the mid-1997 "crisis" countries

5

(Korea, Thailand, Indonesia, and Malaysia), Japan, China, and the smaller, less affected and more resilient economies (Taiwan, Singapore, and Hong Kong).

In the crisis countries between mid-1997 and the end of 1998, the combined effects of currency depreciation and deflated property and equity markets caused asset values to plummet by about 75 percent. An approximate averaging over all of the four Asian crisis economies and currencies indicates that, as a general order of magnitude, an asset in these countries worth $100 in June of 1997 was worth only $25 a year later.

One way of measuring the depth of Asia's economic turmoil is to compare it with historic market crashes in the United States. In the period from 1929 to 1932, the Standard & Poor's Index decreased by about 87 percent, in 1962 by about 28 percent, and in 1987 by about 34 percent.

By the middle of 1999 (the time of this writing), Korea and Thailand were no longer in crisis, although they had not completed the recovery and restructuring process. Both countries had reversed the negative GDP growth of the two preceding years and realized positive economic growth. Their current accounts were in surplus, foreign exchange reserves increased, and foreign direct investment resumed—substantially in Korea and modestly in Thailand. In Indonesia and Malaysia, progress was discernible, but more limited than in Korea and Thailand. Currency and other asset values rose substantially in Malaysia (at least temporarily buoyed by capital controls). Indonesia's economic prospects were deeply mired in the country's political uncertainties, although there was a modest resumption of foreign direct investment.

In sum, while the record thus far and prospects of continued recovery are stronger in Korea and Thailand than in Malaysia and Indonesia, in general, the region's crisis is behind it. Moreover, while recovery in the four crisis countries was previously thought to depend on Japan's recovery, their recovery is well ahead of that of Japan. Our forecasts for Korea and Indonesia, summarized in Chapters Three and Four, reflect this judgment.

JAPAN

The serious economic problems besetting Japan predate and transcend the mid-1997 financial crisis elsewhere in East Asia; indeed, Japan's economic problems have been only marginally affected by that crisis. As will be discussed more fully in succeeding chapters, Japan's economic problems are structural rather than cyclical. They are reflected by an annualized GDP growth rate in the 1990s of about 1 percent, compared with a growth rate in the 1980s nearly four times larger.

Nevertheless, Japan maintains a high level of per-capita GDP—between $43,000 and $23,000 currently—depending, respectively, on whether nominal or real purchasing-power-parity rates are used to convert Japanese yen into U.S. dollars. Also, Japan maintains the largest current account surplus (estimated at more than $120 billion in 1999), and the largest foreign exchange reserves (over $225 billion) of any economy in the world.

Japan's efforts to reform and restructure its economy will be assessed more fully later in this report. That assessment is reflected in the forecasts for the Japanese economy summarized in Chapters Three and Four. In effect, the high per-capita GDP and large foreign exchange reserves provide a form of protection and insulation for Japan that enables it to pursue a very gradual—some might even say leisurely—pace of economic reform, and to avoid the painful restructuring that would be necessary to enhance the economy's performance.

CHINA

China, like Japan, has thus far been only marginally affected by the financial crisis elsewhere in Asia. Nevertheless, the economic picture presented by China is mixed and decidedly different from the situations prevailing elsewhere in Asia.

On the positive side, and despite a wide range of sometimes fuzzy statistics, China maintains a high rate of GDP growth—probably less than its reported rate of 7 to 7.8 percent, but probably in the range of 5 to 6 percent per annum. Also on the positive side, China's current account is substantially in surplus (nearly $30 billion in the most recent 12-month period), and the foreign direct investment (FDI) it receives from abroad (an annual rate of $30–35 billion) is the largest among the emerging market countries. Even though exports and FDI are below peak levels, they remain large and strong. China's foreign exchange reserves, at over $150 billion, are second only to those of Japan among the world's economies. Another positive indication for China's future is the largely completed "buy out" by the government of the Chinese Army's commercial enterprises with a view toward their early privatization.

Yet, China also displays a nearly equal array of negative indicators, including its thousands of inefficient and loss-incurring state-owned enterprises (SOEs) whose continuing deficits impose an enormous burden on the banking system that finances their deficits. As a result, the Chinese economy is riven by a pervasive misallocation of credit between the favored but nonperforming state sector and the disfavored-but-generally-more-efficient nonstate sector. The government's overarching fear of increased urban unemployment and possible social unrest impedes the pace and prospects for reform of the SOEs.

TAIWAN, SINGAPORE, HONG KONG

Finally, the smaller and more resilient economies of Taiwan, Singapore, and Hong Kong provide still another part of the East Asian mosaic, differing from the rest of the region as well as displaying differences among themselves.

Each of these cases is different—for example, Taiwan and Singapore have maintained a flexible exchange rate system, while Hong Kong has a fixed-peg currency board. Since the mid-1997 crisis in East Asia, Hong Kong's asset bubble in property and equity markets has popped, which in turn has resulted in negative growth for the economy as a whole. Singapore and Taiwan have been less affected, and both maintained or resumed positive growth rates by the middle of 1999, while Hong Kong showed distinct signs of moving in this direction.

Chapter Three

PRINCIPAL FORECAST RESULTS

METHODS AND DATA

As noted earlier, the forecasting model used in this study is the same as that used in our 1995 estimates,[1] and similar to that used in our 1989 work.[2] The model is a macroeconomic, supply-side (capacity) series of equations that links the growth of GDP to growth of employed labor, capital, and productivity, and then in turn links military spending to GDP growth, and military investment and military capital to military spending.

The model serves as an accounting device for identifying specific elements (i.e., inputs) that affect GDP growth, military spending, and military investment as outputs. The key parameters used in the model have been established by calculating their actual average (mean) values and variances over the decade prior to the 1997 financial turmoil, and superimposing on these values the authors' judgments about whether, why, and by how much the parameters will change over the 2000–2015 period.

In most cases, the parameter values we use are close to (i.e., within one standard deviation of) the generally stable averages of the decade prior to the 1997–1998 Asian financial troubles. In those cases where we depart from this practice, the basis for these departures is explained in the accompanying text and in Appendix B. The judgments that we make are thus informed by the historical trends

---

[1] See Wolf et al., 1995, and Appendix A for a description of the model.

[2] Wolf et al., 1989.

but not confined by them. Appendix B includes a comparison of the historical means and variances of the parameters with the values used in making our forecasts, together with brief explanations of the reasoning behind the authors' judgments.

It goes without saying that the resulting forecasts are subject to major uncertainties that could appreciably alter the parameter values. We regard our parameter estimates, and the forecasts that result from them, as plausible central tendencies. However, many exogenous circumstances—for example, civil unrest, international financial crises, local wars—could significantly change these values.[3] In the separate forecasts for China and India, the multiplicity of uncertainties for these two countries is reflected by positing two sharply different scenarios encompassing different states of the world. The alternative scenarios generate very different results. For the other three countries—Japan, Korea, and Indonesia—the uncertainties surrounding the forecasts are briefly indicated in the text accompanying each country's forecast, rather than by specifying alternative scenarios.[4]

In this chapter, we summarize the principal results in terms of the four key indicators—GDP, per-capita GDP, military spending, and military investment and military capital stock—for the five countries, Japan, China, India, Korea, and Indonesia. Like the earlier work, the method we use does not deal with possible interactive effects of changes in one country on other countries. Such interactions may be especially important for the parameter γ, representing the share of GDP devoted to military spending. As indicated in Appendix B, this parameter was remarkably stable during the referenced decade, reflecting both the prevalence of peace in the region and the durability of organizational pressures and claims in the budgetary processes of the individual countries. Consequently, our forecasts typically as-

---

[3]One of the great advantages of the simple aggregate model we have used is its transparency. If readers believe that the parameter values we employ are wide of the mark, other values can be readily substituted to generate forecasts.

[4]One of the reviewers of an earlier draft of this study urged the authors to elaborate on what the forecasts do and do not suggest. The above text explicates what the forecasts are intended to suggest. They do not suggest that the estimates have been made by an econometric exercise using a complex, multisector model, nor one that might try to take account "of changed political and cultural circumstances" (to quote the reviewer's comments).

sume constancy, or near constancy, of the military share in each of the countries.

The current forecasts are based on the use of more recent and better data from both official and nonofficial sources than were available in our earlier work. These sources are cited and described in the separate sections in Chapter Four dealing with the individual countries.

However, various possible external and internal developments could trigger significant departures from the historical patterns, and from the judgments we have made about potential changes in the key parameters. For example, as indicated in Chapter Five, the progress of successful military modernization in China, or continued missile development in North Korea, could stimulate a significant rise in Japan's military spending. Contrariwise, resource pressures in China, or diminished political influence of the military in Indonesia, could result in substantial reductions in military spending in these countries.

The results are reported in terms of both nominal exchange rates (XR) and purchasing-power-parity (PPP) rates. In the case of the military investment component of military spending, we use a separate PPP rate pertaining to the costs of purchasing investment goods (PI), while the aggregate PPP rate is used for converting the remaining majority of total military spending covering pay and allowances, operations, and maintenance. The military capital stock estimates thus reflect use of the PI rate (for investment goods), because the military capital estimates are constructed from the individual military investment portion of military spending, minus depreciation of the previously accumulated military capital stock.

To interpret the frequently quite different estimates resulting from using nominal XR and real PPP rates, it is important to recognize that each of these rates provides an answer to a different question:

* Use of the nominal exchange rate for conversions from constant prices in local currencies answers the following question: How many dollars are *required* to exchange into local currency (i.e., yen, RMB, rupees, etc.) at a specified nominal exchange rate in order to *buy* the GDP market-basket (of Japan, China, India, etc.) with local currency at *local* prices?

- Use of the PPP exchange rate for conversion of local currencies to dollars answers a different question: How many dollars would be *received* if the same market-basket were *sold* (i.e., valued) at U.S. prices?

Although there is a tendency for nominal (XR) and real (PPP) rates to converge, the process of convergence is slow and imperfect.[5] The principal impediments to convergence are the huge volume as well as volatility of international capital movements, which principally affect nominal XR rather than PPPs, and the large, but perhaps diminishing, volume of nontradable goods and services, which principally affect real (PPP) rates rather than nominal rates. Where prices of nontraded goods and services are low (as in China) relative to the corresponding ones in other countries (such as Japan), the PPP rate will exceed the nominal XR; and conversely, when prices of nontraded goods and services are high (as in Japan), the nominal XR will exceed the PPP rate.

One result of the differing forces impinging on nominal and real exchange rates is that nominal rates are, under a regime of flexible exchange rates, enormously more volatile and transitory than real PPP rates. For example, between 1998 and 1999, the Japanese yen appreciated by more than 20 percent relative to the U.S. dollar, while between 1997 and 1998 Korea's won and Indonesia's rupiah depreciated by 50–80 percent, respectively, relative to the dollar; their corresponding PPP rates changed very little. Consequently, use of nominal exchange rates is especially hazardous in attempting to make intercountry comparisons.[6]

---

[5]See Prakash Apte, Marian Kane, and Peit Sercu, "Relative Purchasing Power Parity and the Medium Run," *Journal of International Money and Finance*, Vol. 13, No. 4, October 1994; and Kenneth Froot and Kenneth Rogoff, "Perspective on PPP and Long Run Real Exchange Rates," in *Handbook of International Economics*, G. M. Grossman and K. Rogoff, eds., North Holland, 1995.

[6]For readers mainly concerned with comparing the relative economic size of countries or their respective standards of living, the PPP estimates are more relevant than the XR estimates.

For readers mainly interested in national security issues, the choice is less clear and more complicated. PPP estimates tend to overstate the equivalent dollar value of military spending and military capital in local currency in less-developed countries (e.g., China, India, Korea, and Indonesia) and understate it in more-developed countries (e.g., Japan). However, XR estimates have the reverse effects: understating military

It is also worth noting, and will become evident in the results reported in this study, that in general the PPP value of a country's currency is larger relative to its nominal exchange rate in emerging-market countries than in advanced industrialized countries because of the higher proportion of nontradables in the former's national output. For example, the PPP of China's RMB in terms of U.S. dollars is four or five times greater than the RMB's nominal exchange rate, while the PPP of the Japanese yen is only about half that of its nominal exchange value.

GROSS DOMESTIC PRODUCT

Table 1 summarizes actual GDP levels for 1995, and our forecasts for the period from 2000 to 2015 for the five countries, using both XR and PPP conversion rates. Figure 1 depicts these estimates in PPP terms.

As Table 1 indicates, it makes a great deal of difference whether GDP is expressed in terms of nominal exchange rates or purchasing-power-parity rates. For Japan, the PPP value of the yen is 87 percent less than the nominal exchange rate value of the yen. Consequently,

---

spending and military capital in less-developed countries, and overstating that of developed countries. To resolve this conundrum, it would be reasonable to evaluate in PPP terms the preponderant part of military spending devoted to services, other nontradables, and domestically produced military equipment, while using XR conversion rates for the portion of military capital outlays devoted to imported military equipment. Imported military equipment in Japan, China, India, Korea, and Indonesia represents about 16 percent, 5 percent, 12 percent, 33 percent, and nearly 100 percent, respectively. (These figures on military deliveries are for 1998 from *The Military Balance*, International Institute of Strategic Studies, 1999–2000, in combination with our estimates of total military procurement.) To avoid the complexity of this approach, in this study we follow and recommend an alternative procedure. This procedure evaluates total military spending in PPP terms while evaluating outlays for military investment (which increment the stock of military capital) in terms of the purchasing power of local currencies for investment goods only, as distinct from the full market-basket of goods and services encompassed in the broad PPP index. The rationale for this procedure is that the index for investment goods (denoted as PI, rather than PPP) generally lies between XR and PPP rates in both less-developed and developed countries. Domestic prices of investment goods generally are closer to international prices (because large proportions of these goods are internationally traded) than are the domestic prices of nontradable goods and services that dominate the broad PPP index.

While this procedure is recommended, we nevertheless include both XR and PPP estimates in our forecasts.

Table 1

Gross Domestic Products of Selected Countries, 1995–2015
(in trillions (10^{12}) of 1998 U.S. dollars)

	1995	2000	2005	2010	2015	Average Annual Growth Rates, 2000–2015 (%)
Nominal exchange rates (XR)						
Japan	5.5	5.5	5.8	6.3	6.8	1.4
China						
A: Stable growth	0.9	1.2	1.5	1.9	2.5	5
B: Disrupted growth	0.9	1.2	1.4	1.6	1.9	2.7
India	0.4	0.5	0.6	0.8	1.1	5.8
Korea	0.3	0.3	0.4	0.6	0.8	5.6
Indonesia	0.06	0.06	0.08	0.09	0.1	4.2
Purchasing-power parity (PPP)						
Japan	2.9	2.9	3.1	3.4	3.6	1.4
China						
A: Stable growth	4.5	6.0	7.6	9.6	12.4	5
B: Disrupted growth	4.5	5.7	6.8	7.7	8.5	2.7
India	2.2	3.0	4.0	5.2	6.7	5.8
Korea	0.7	0.7	0.9	1.2	1.7	5.6
Indonesia	0.7	0.7	0.9	1.1	1.4	4.2

NOTE: The sources are shown in Chapter Four.

our estimate for GDP in Japan in 2015 is $6.8 trillion in terms of 1998 dollars, while in PPP terms the corresponding figure is only $3.6 trillion.

China provides a sharp contrast. The relationship between the exchange rate and PPP estimates in Japan is turned on its head in China: China's GDP is $2.5 trillion in XR terms, while the estimate is $12.4 trillion in PPP terms.

For the entire period from 2000 to 2015, Japan's GDP growth rate is slightly above that for the preceding decade, rising from 1.1 percent in the period 2000–2005 to 1.6 percent in the period 2010–2015. While the forecast for Japan's growth is slightly lower than that in our 1995 report, that report showed a falling trend in Japan's growth while the current forecast shows a slightly rising one.

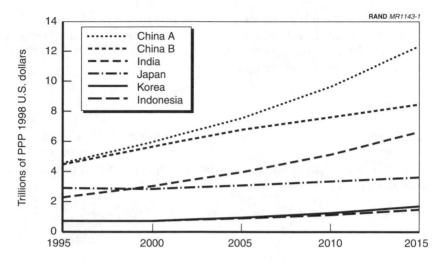

NOTE: Based on PPP rates for converting local currencies to U.S. dollars.

Figure 1—Gross Domestic Products of Selected Countries, 2000–2015

The GDP estimates for China show a doubling by 2015 in the stable growth scenario (A), and an increase in GDP of only 56 percent in Scenario B. By 2015, China's GDP is more than three times that of Japan in PPP terms, but only 36 percent of Japan's if the nominal exchange rate is used for conversion to dollars. In Scenario B, China's GDP is less than 28 percent of Japan's in nominal XR terms.

India's GDP more than doubles by 2015 in PPP terms, reaching a level of $6.7 trillion U.S. 1998 dollars, about 55 percent of China's in China's Scenario A, and nearly 80 percent of China's in Scenario B, compared with less than half that of China's GDP in 1995.

Korea's GDP growth is estimated as resuming in 2000 (indeed, positive growth already resumed in 1999), rising monotonically to about 6 percent annually, still relatively high although not up to the unusually buoyant rates of the early 1990s. Korea's GDP grows relative to Japan: from 25 percent of Japan's GDP in 2000 to 46 percent by 2015 in PPP terms.

In Indonesia, there is an order-of-magnitude difference between the exchange rate and PPP conversions, still reflecting the currency depreciation of 80 percent between 1996 and 1998. By 2005, Indonesia's real GDP will return to its 1996 level.

PER-CAPITA GDP

Our forecasts for per-capita GDP in both nominal and real exchange rates result from combining the GDP estimates shown in Table 1 with estimates from other sources for the population and population growth rates of the five countries as shown in Table 2.

Table 3 shows the corresponding per-capita GDPs.

Several interesting points from Table 3 are worth highlighting:

*   Notwithstanding Japan's low rate of GDP growth, all the GDP increases are reflected in increased per-capita GDP, because the Japanese population decreases slightly during the period from 2000–2015.

*   China's per-capita GDP doubles by 2015 in PPP terms, although still remaining below $10 thousand.

*   India's per-capita GDP, again in PPP terms, increases slightly relative to that of China, reaching $5.1 thousand, nearly 60 percent of China's in 2015.

Table 2

1995 Populations and 1995–2015 Population Growth Rates

Country	1995 Population (in millions)	Growth Rate 1995–2015 (%/yr)
Japan	126	0
China	1,205	0.86
India	936	1.68
Korea	45	0.6
Indonesia	195	1.1

SOURCES: *Japan Statistical Yearbook*, Tokyo, 1998; *China, Higher Education Publishing House*, Beijing, 1996; United Nations, *World Population Report*, New York, 1998.

Table 3

Per-Capita GDPs of Selected Countries
(in thousands of 1998 U.S. dollars)

	1995	2000	2005	2010	2015
Nominal exchange rates (XR)					
Japan	43.4	43.7	45.5	49.2	53.8
China					
A: Stable growth	0.7	0.9	1.1	1.4	1.7
B: Disrupted Growth	0.7	0.9	1.0	1.2	1.3
India	0.4	0.5	0.6	0.7	0.8
Korea	6.8	7.3	8.6	11.3	15.1
Indonesia	0.3	0.3	0.3	0.4	0.5
Purchasing-power parity (PPP)					
Japan	23.2	23.3	24.4	26.3	28.7
China:					
A: Stable growth	3.7	4.6	5.7	6.9	8.7
B: Disrupted growth	3.7	4.4	5.1	5.5	6.0
India	2.4	2.9	3.5	4.3	5.1
Korea	14.7	15.9	18.6	24.4	32.8
Indonesia	3.7	3.5	4.0	4.7	5.5

NOTE: The sources are shown in Chapter Four.

- Korea's per-capita GDP more than doubles over the 2000–2015 period, exceeding that of Japan in PPP terms by 2015, although still far below Japan's in terms of nominal exchange rates.

- Indonesia's per-capita GDP increases by nearly 60 percent in PPP terms from the post-1997 financial turmoil, although still remaining only slightly higher than that of India ($5.5 thousand in per-capita GDP for Indonesia, compared with $5.1 thousand for India).

The estimates shown in Table 3 are shown graphically in Figure 2.

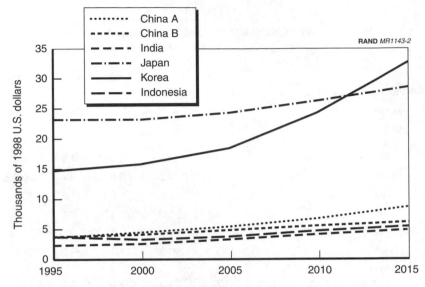

NOTE: Based on PPP rates for converting local currencies to U.S. dollars.

Figure 2—Per-Capita GDPs of Selected Countries

MILITARY SPENDING

The military spending estimates for the five countries are derived from their corresponding GDP estimates by applying a parameter, γ, representing the expected share of GDP devoted to military spending in each country. As explained in Appendix B, this parameter has been estimated from each country's experience in the past decade combined with our judgments about changes that may be expected to occur during the 2000–2015 period. The following are the values for the military spending-shares that we have used: Japan, 1.1 percent; China, 2–3 percent; India, 4 percent; Korea, 3.5 percent; and Indonesia, 1.8–2 percent.

The resulting military spending estimates are summarized in Table 4.

Several salient points emerge from the XR and PPP estimates shown in Table 4 and the PPP curves in Figure 3:

Table 4

Military Spending Estimates
(in billions of 1998 U.S. dollars)

	1995	2000	2005	2010	2015
Nominal exchange rates (XR)					
Japan	52.3	60.9	63.9	69.1	74.8
China[a]					
A: Stable growth	18–27	24–36	31–46	39–59	51–75
B: Disrupted growth	18	23	27	31	35
India	10.3	16.8	25.4	33.3	42.9
Korea	10.1	11.4	13.5	18.2	24.9
Indonesia	1.1	1.1	1.5	1.8	2.3
Purchasing-power parity (PPP)					
Japan	27.9	32.6	34.2	36.9	39.9
China[a]					
A: Stable growth	90–135	120–180	152–228	192–288	249–373
B: Disrupted growth	90	115	136	154	171
India	64.1	105.0	158.1	207.0	267.0
Korea	21.9	24.7	29.1	39.3	53.9
Indonesia	13.0	13.5	18.1	22.5	27.8

[a]The spread of the estimates for China in the "stable growth" scenario results from using values for the military spending share, γ, between 2 percent and 3 percent of GDP. In the "disrupted growth" scenario, γ remains fixed at 2 percent.

NOTE: The sources are shown in Chapter Four.

- While Japan's military spending rises by about 22 percent in the period from 2000 to 2015, its military spending falls relative to that of China. However, if nominal exchange rates are used, Japan's military spending remains above China's, but is substantially below China's if PPP rates are used for converting local currencies to dollar equivalents.

- India's military spending during the period from 2000–2015 rises substantially relative to that of China, increasing from about 58 percent of China's military spending in PPP terms in the year 2000 to about 85 percent of China's in 2015.

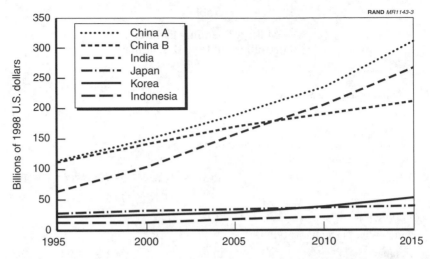

NOTE: Based on PPP rates for converting local currencies to U.S. dollars.

Figure 3—Military Spending Estimates

MILITARY CAPITAL

The estimates of military capital—the cumulation of annual military investment in weapons and procurement, net of depreciation on the previously accumulated capital stock—were built up recursively, starting with the 1995 estimates in our previous work. The military capital estimates for 1995 in this prior work were adjusted in several ways: using the most recent (1995) Penn World Tables for the purchasing-power parities for investment goods (PI) in local currencies in each of the five countries, rather than aggregate PPP adjustments; shifting the base year from 1994 to 1998 U.S. dollars; expressing the resulting estimates in terms of both nominal exchange rates and purchasing-power equivalents for investment goods (PI); and adding increments to the stock of military capital since 1994, based on annual new military investment (procurement of weapons and military construction) through 2015, *minus* depreciation of the previously accumulated military capital stock.

To build the new capital stock estimates, we apply a parameter (π) to the annual military spending estimates, representing the share of military spending devoted to new military investment (i.e., military procurement), less the annual depreciation rate, δ, applied to the previously accumulated military capital figures. As explained in Appendix B, the respective country values of π (the military capital share of military spending) are based on recent experience combined with assumptions and judgments about the corresponding values in the future. The following are the values of the capital share, π, used in the estimates and derived from analysis of the corresponding national budgets and other sources: Japan, 21 percent; China, 25–32 percent; India, 25 percent; Korea, 30 percent; and Indonesia, 25 percent.

In each case, we apply an annual depreciation rate of 10 percent for all military capital accumulated through 1994, and a lower depreciation rate of 8 percent for new military investment acquired in 1995 and later years. The underlying assumption behind these differential depreciation rates, δ, is that military equipment procured in earlier years depreciates more rapidly because of technological advancement embodied in later-vintage military systems, while newer procurements depreciate more slowly.

It should be emphasized that military capital is hardly a reliable proxy for effective military power, anymore than aggregate GDP is a reliable proxy for economic power. Clearly, other factors such as command and control, training and morale, leadership, logistic support, and intelligence have major and often decisive influences on effective military power, quite apart from the size and current value of military capital. Still, the accumulation of military capital stocks represents one relevant dimension of effective military power.[7] This, plus the feasibility of measuring it, accounts for the attention we devote to military capital.

Our estimates and forecasts of military capital stocks for the five countries from 1995–2015 are summarized in Table 5. The estimates shown in Table 5 are reproduced in Figure 4.

---

[7]See the discussion in Chapter Five.

Table 5

Military Capital Stocks of Selected Asian Countries
(in billions of 1998 U.S. dollars)

	1995	2000	2005	2010	2015
Nominal exchange rates (XR)					
Japan	173.4	154.3	149.7	156.4	165.8
China					
A: Stable growth[a]	63.0	69–78	84–106	106–138	135–182
B: Disrupted growth	63.0	69	82	97	113
India	29.0	32.2	43.8	60.5	96.9
Korea	25.4	30.8	35.3	43.5	56.9
Indonesia	5.0	4.1	4.0	4.3	5.0
Purchasing-power parity (PI)[a]					
Japan	124.4	111.5	107.4	112.2	118.9
China					
A: Stable growth[b]	217.0	241–276	295–339	372–485	478–534
B: Disrupted growth	217.0	238	282	333	464
India	112.0	124.2	169.1	233.6	314.0
Korea	55.0	61.4	70.4	86.8	113.5
Indonesia	46.6	38.9	37.3	40.6	47.3

[a]PI represents the purchasing-power parity for investment goods, as distinct from aggregate PPP for the GDP as a whole.

[b]The range of the military capital estimates for China in Scenario A results from the assumption that defense spending as a share of GDP might vary between 2 percent and 3 percent.

NOTE: The sources are shown in Chapter Four.

Several significant points emerge from the results summarized in Table 5 and Figure 4:

- Japan's military capital appears to fall during the first ten years of the new century because annual military investments—which our model links to Japan's slow rate of GDP growth—are less than depreciations from the previously accumulated capital stock. Military capital begins to grow again in the period 2010–2015, although at the end of 2015, Japan's military capital is still below what it was in 1995. This is an artifact of our one-country-

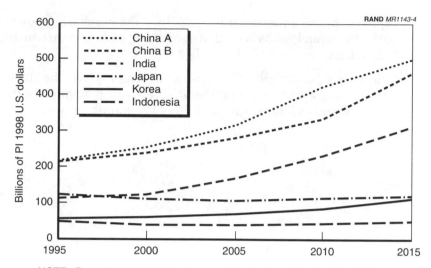

NOTE: Based on purchasing-power parities for investment goods (PI) in converting from local currencies to U.S. dollars.

Figure 4—Military Capital Stocks of Selected Asian Countries

at-a-time method of analysis, which unrealistically neglects the interactive effects on Japan's own military investment of the probable buildup in China, Korea, and elsewhere.

- China's military capital stock nearly doubles between 2000 and 2015. If nominal exchange rates are used for conversion from constant-price yuan to 1998 dollars, China's military capital stock by 2015 is about the same as that of Japan. However, if the calculations are based on the more appropriate conversion rate for the purchasing power of the yuan for investment goods, then China's military capital is more than twice that of Japan by the end of the 2015 period.

- Using the PI conversion rate, India's military capital rises over the 2000–2015 period by two-and-one-half times, and by 2015 it reaches a level of over $300 billion, nearly two-thirds that of China, compared with only half that of China in the year 2000.

- Korea's military capital increases by 85 percent over the 2000–2015 period, rising from less than 60 percent of Japan's military capital to nearly equal the latter by 2015, if the purchasing-power parity for capital goods is used in converting from Korean won to U.S. dollars.

- Indonesia's military capital increases very slightly over the 2000–2015 period, again reflecting the link between new military investment and Indonesia's modest rate of economic growth.

Chapter Four

ESTIMATES FOR THE FIVE COUNTRIES, 2000–2015

A COMMENT ON THE ESTIMATING MODEL

As noted in Chapter Three, the estimating model we use is set forth in Appendix A. Estimates of the key input variables and model parameters are derived from multiple official and nonofficial unclassified data for the 1980–1998 period. The forecasts use the calculated mean parameter values or their time trends, or adjust these calculated values based on the authors' explicit reasons for doing so.[1]

The estimates presented for each country are in 1998 U.S. dollars. For each country, the original calculations are in terms of constant 1995 values in local currencies, which are then converted to 1998 U.S. dollar values using the latest Penn World Tables (version 5.7) through the mid-1990s, estimated for both nominal exchange rates and purchasing-power-parity values. Adjustments in the 1995 nominal exchange rates are based on the separate PPP values for the gross national products of each country and for the capital goods component of their GDPs—the latter serving as a proxy for the PPP rates applicable to military investments.

JAPAN

As noted in the preceding discussion of Asia's financial troubles, Japan's economic problems are structural rather than cyclical. This implies that changes will continue to be difficult and slow. In turn,

---

[1]See Appendix B.

our forecasts for Japan are heavily influenced by the record of the 1990s and envisage only a gradual improvement in that record from 2000 to 2015.

The structural aspects of the Japanese economy that constrain its resurgence include the following:

*   An industrial system principally driven by considerations of scale, market share, and exports; profitability has typically been viewed as less important in resource allocation and in the development of industries and firms.

*   A banking system still pervaded by nonperforming and otherwise fragile loans resulting from this distorted industrial base and the credit misallocations associated with it.

*   A regulatory system marked by the heavy hand of government, limiting free entry and market access both within the Japanese economy and from potentially competitive firms outside of it, in the process tending to stifle entrepreneurship and innovation.[2]

*   Perverse demographic trends resulting in a rapidly aging population, a declining ratio between Japanese of prime working ages and retirees, and a highly restrictive immigration policy that precludes one possible source of relief from these trends, while continued social constraints on women in the work place inhibit another.

To mitigate these structural difficulties, Japan has embarked on three principal reform policies: loosened monetary policies that include government bailout funding for the major banks, thereby strengthening their balance sheets and facilitating new lending; increasing levels of public spending (in the process, further expanding Japan's large public debt, which is already larger than its

---

[2]These structural rigidities are reflected in recent work at RAND which attempts to measure the relative degree of economic "openness" of different economies. One of the principal findings is that the economy of Japan ranks far below the economies of the United States and Germany (the latter as a proxy for the European Union—EU), and is roughly similar to China and Korea in terms of the nontariff barriers to economic openness that permeate the economy and impede market access by foreign businesses. See Charles Wolf, Jr., Hugh Levaux, and Daochi Tong, *Economic Openness: Many Facets, Many Metrics,* Santa Monica, Calif.: RAND, MR-1072-SRF, 1999.

GDP); and providing a modest degree of deregulation (for example, in financial services), and allowing foreign investors to acquire Japanese assets in some fields.

Most observers, including the authors of this report, believe these efforts are insufficient to deal with the economy's fundamental problems. Without more drastic deregulation, Japan's near stagnation is likely to continue.

Yet, Japan is hardly in a "crisis" condition. Its per-capita GDP remains among the highest in the world. Sales of luxury consumer goods carrying the prestige labels of Vuiton, Gucci, and Hermes continue to rise. Japan's current account surplus (about $120 billion at an annual rate in 1999), and its foreign exchange reserves (over $225 billion) are the world's largest. Although protracted stagnation has doubled Japan's unemployment rate (to about 4.6 percent), this is less than half that prevailing in the European Union.[3] Under these circumstances, Japan's political system and its successive leaderships remain reluctant to expose the economy to the disruptive stimulus of genuinely opening its economy to competition from abroad as well as from potential entrepreneurial activity at home.

Several key aspects of Japan's recent economic data are important both for understanding these structural problems and for providing a basis for the forecasts summarized below:[4]

- From 1990 to 1995, the ratio of public to private capital formation steadily increased from 33 percent to 57 percent, and this trend continued in the latter part of the 1990s.

- Over the same period, the absolute level of private capital formation declined by 12 percent (from ¥85 trillion to ¥75 trillion, in constant 1995 prices), while capital formation in the public sector increased by 50 percent (from ¥28 trillion to ¥43 trillion). The same pattern has persisted through the second half of the 1990s.

---

[3]Admittedly, unemployment rates in Japan and the EU are not strictly comparable, among other reasons because of the long-standing and extensive unemployment entitlements in the EU, but not in Japan.

[4]The points made in the text are all derived from the *Japan Statistical Yearbook*, 1998 (Tokyo, Japan, and additional data provided in the Ministry of Finance's web page http://www.mof.go.jp/english).

- The incremental capital/output ratio increased from 2.3 in the period from 1980 to 1985, to 3.7 from 1985 to 1990, to a strikingly high figure of 15.8 in the 1990–1995 period.

- Again, in the same period, the labor share in national income increased monotonically from 60 to 67 percent in terms of income at market prices, and from 67 to 73 percent in terms of factor cost; hence, the capital (nonwage income) share has correspondingly declined.

To be sure, these data on capital formation and income shares can be interpreted in both counter-cyclical and in structural terms. The counter-cyclical interpretation for the declining level of private capital formation follows from Japan's protracted stagnation: Incentives for private investment have diminished, and government spending on infrastructure and other public programs has been rising in an attempt to stimulate the economy. The alternative structural interpretation is that productivity and profitability of private investment in Japan have been largely confined to export sectors, while they have been declining for domestic production and service sectors. Contributing to these declines have been impediments to entry by new firms, absence of or limited access to venture capital, and scarcity and lack of openness and credit for new entrepreneurs. Both the cyclical and structural interpretations are relevant. However, the protracted character of the several indicators strongly suggests that the principal explanation is structural rather than cyclical—cyclical stagnation typically does not endure for a decade.

Finally, annual total factor productivity (TFP) growth between 1980 and 1995 averaged 0.5 percent; from 1985 to 1990 annual TFP growth was 1.4 percent, while from 1990 to 1995 the corresponding TFP growth figure was *negative* 2.1 percent! In turn, this sharp decrease in factor productivity contributes to the decreased ratio of private capital formation to public capital formation, and the increased capital/output ratio mentioned earlier.

Table 6 summarizes our estimates for the four key variables (GDP, per-capita GDP, military spending, and military capital), covering the period from 1995 through 2015. All of the estimates are in 1998 U.S. dollars, evaluated in terms of nominal exchange rates, purchasing-power-parity rates, and, in the case of military capital, in terms of the purchasing power of the yen for investment goods.

The information summarized in Table 6 is also presented graphically in Figures 5–8.

Several critical assumptions, on which the forecasts summarized in Table 6 and Figures 5–8 depend, should be highlighted:

- The forecasts include the judgment that the key total factor productivity parameter (τ), while rising from the negative figure of –2.1 percent per year in the mid-1990s, will improve only slightly in the next decade, reaching a positive 0.4 percent annual figure in the period 2010–2015. This judgment assumes that the pace of deregulation and reform in Japan will be slow and partial, largely for political and social rather than economic reasons. If this assumption turns out to be wide of the mark, and major liberalization occurs rapidly, the forecast for Japan would be considerably increased.

- Japan's military spending is assumed to remain at 1.1 percent of GDP. This assumption may be sensitive to the progress of defense spending and military modernization in China, as well as to the unpredictable behavior of North Korea. Either of these external conditioning factors could plausibly trigger an increase in Japan's military spending.

If the uncertainties embedded in these assumptions evolve differently from our prognoses, the outcomes could diverge appreciably from the forecasts.

We have also assumed that the rate of depreciation of military capital accumulated up to and including 1994 is 10 percent annually, while more-recent military investment from 1995 to 2015 would depreciate at an 8 percent annual rate. The rationale for these assumptions is that advances in military technology (including the "revolution in military affairs") tend to accelerate obsolescence of older economic systems, thereby warranting a higher depreciation rate for military capital accumulated prior to 1994.

Given the foregoing assumptions, several key points can be drawn from Table 6 and Figures 5–8.

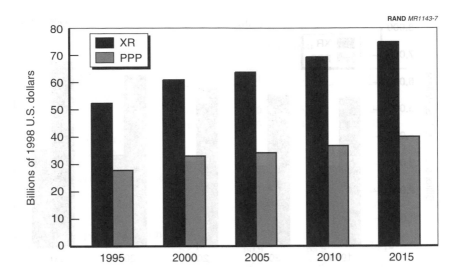

Figure 7—Japan Trends: Military Spending

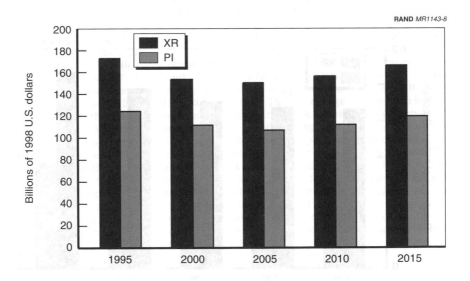

Figure 8—Japan Trends: Military Capital

First, it makes a great difference whether we calculate these four variables in terms of nominal exchange rates, purchasing-power parity in the aggregate, or, in the case of military capital, purchasing-power parity for investment goods. For Japan, the PPP value of the yen used in our estimates is 87 percent less than its nominal exchange value, while the purchasing-power parity of the yen for investment goods is only 48 percent less than that of the nominal exchange rate.[5] Consequently, our estimate for GDP in Japan in 2015 is $6.8 trillion in terms of 1998 dollars using the XR conversion rate, while the corresponding figure is only $3.6 trillion if PPP rates are applied.

Second, the forecasted annual growth rate for the Japanese economy in the period 2000–2005 is just below 1 percent, increasing to 1.56 percent in the 2005–2010 period, and to 1.62 percent for the following five-year period.

Third, over the 15 years covered by these forecasts, per-capita GDP in Japan rises from about $44 thousand to $54 thousand in XR terms, or from $23 thousand to $29 thousand in terms of PPP.

Fourth, for military spending, the estimate for 2000 is approximately $61 billion rising to $75 billion in 2015 in XR terms, and from $33 billion in 2000 to $40 billion in 2015 in PPP terms.

Finally, the military capital figures are estimated in terms of three different conversion rates: nominal exchange rates, purchasing-power parity in the aggregate, and purchasing-power parity of the yen for investment goods. Most Japanese military systems are purchased at prices reflecting world market prices in dollars, or at yen prices reflecting those of investment goods, rather than of consumption goods. Consequently the purchasing-power parity for investment goods is probably the most reliable of the three estimates. On this basis, Japan's military capital stock can be expected to increase from about $112 billion in 2000 to $119 billion in 2015, based on the assumptions we have made about accelerated depreciation of the systems acquired before 1994, and the lower depreciation rate for

---

[5]According to the most recent (1994) estimates in the Penn World Tables (5.7 preliminary version) the XR, PPP, and PI values are ¥95, ¥176, and ¥139, per U.S. dollar, respectively.

systems acquired thereafter. Once again, these estimates exclude the possible interactive effects of developments in China as well as in North Korea that might significantly alter Japanese priorities with respect to resource allocations for the military.[6]

CHINA

Before summarizing the forecasts for China, several key assumptions underlying the GDP estimates should be noted. We have adjusted the official GDP statistics because of a belief that the State Statistical Bureau (SSB) has substantially underestimated the size of China's GDP and significantly overestimated its growth rate.

Underestimation of GDP in the official statistics results from the incomplete statistical coverage of economic activities in the service sector and in rural areas, especially in earlier years. Examples include services in the informal economy that are provided by traders, carpenters, repairs persons, alternative medicine practitioners, and

---

[6]Several salient differences between the forecasts made in our earlier work (Wolf et al., 1995) and those shown in Table 6 and Figures 5–8 should be noted. First, the current forecasts are expressed in 1998 dollars, using both nominal exchange rates and real purchasing-power-parity rates, while the earlier estimates were expressed in 1994 dollars using only PPP for conversion from the Japanese yen. Second, the yen's PPP value used in our current report is approximately 15 percent higher than that used in the earlier work, and the U.S. GDP deflator rose by 8 percent between 1994 and 1998; hence, expressing our results in 1998 dollars boosts the estimates expressed in 1994 dollars in the earlier work. Third, while the earlier work forecasted an average annual growth rate for the Japanese economy of 2.5 percent in the period from 2000 to 2015, the current forecasts envisage average annual growth of only 1.4 percent over this period. Moreover, the growth trajectory in the earlier work was slightly downward, while the growth trajectory in the current work is slightly upward. The explanation for these differences essentially lies in the sources and duration of Japan's protracted stagnation, as discussed earlier in the text above. Fourth, the GDP estimates in our current work are slightly lower than the corresponding estimates in the earlier work, netting out the offsetting effects of slower growth over the 1994–2000 and 2000–2015 periods on the one hand, and the factors mentioned above that tend to raise the estimates, on the other. Fifth, estimates of per-capita GDP and of military spending shown in the tables and figures above are also slightly below those shown in our earlier work, for the same reasons noted in the fourth point above. And finally, our current forecasts of military capital are appreciably below those shown in our earlier work, for several reasons additional to those mentioned above: use of a lower parameter for new military investment as a percentage of military spending (21 percent versus 27 percent in the earlier work) (see *Defense of Japan*, 1998, Tokyo, for the 21 percent estimate), and higher annual rates of depreciation in the current forecasts compared with those in the earlier 1995 work.

private lenders. Such activities and businesses proliferated as the economy evolved from a planned to a market system: To evade taxation, their output and income have not been fully reported. Another area of undercoverage is farm output and consumption in kind, due to underreporting of farm land. And a third missing item is rural consumption of noncommercial energy sources such as fuel wood, bio gas, and grain stalks.

Another reason for adjusting the official GDP statistics is the undervaluation of certain output and services, including subsidized housing, medical services, education, transportation, and utilities provided to urban residents; artificially low interest rates charged to state-owned enterprises; and home consumption of farm products valued at procurement prices below market prices. While there is also some overestimation of certain components of GDP, such as the output of rural industries, on balance the official GDP statistics are probably still too low.

Estimates of the extent of this underestimation vary widely, covering a range of 16 to 55 percent above the official figure. In our estimates, we assume that the undervaluation is 34 percent, which is the figure used by the World Bank and Angus Maddison.[7]

There are also convincing reasons to believe that the official GDP growth rates have been biased upwards. These include the following contributing factors:

- The deflators used by the SSB to convert nominal to real GDP growth have been too low (for example, the factor price index rose much faster than the implicit deflator for gross value of industrial output in the 1990–1997 period).[8]

- An upward bias is introduced into the aggregate output index as a result of the relatively slower growing state sector being underweighted in the index. This underweighting occurs because many of the state sector's products and services, such as energy,

---

[7]See World Bank, *China GNP Per Capita*, Washington D.C., 1994; Angus Maddison, *Dynamic Forces in Capitalist Development: A Long-Run Comparative Review*, New York: Oxford University Press, 1991.

[8]See World Bank, *China 2020*, Washington, D.C., 1997.

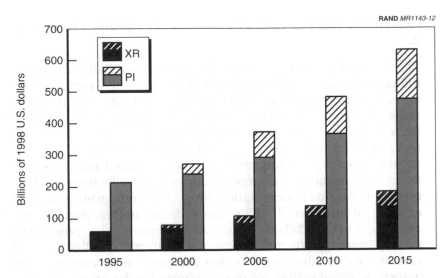

NOTE: The cross-hatching indicates the effects on military investment and military capital of varying the GDP share of military spending between 2 percent and 3 percent annually.

Figure 12—China Trends, 1995–2015: Military Capital
(Scenario A)

of investment goods, the proportion of military investment in military spending (and also, for that matter, in GDP) shrinks.

Several salient points emerge from Tables 7 and 8 for Scenarios A and B, and Figures 9–12 for Scenario A.

- China's GDP approximately doubles from 2000 to 2015 in Scenario A and increases by nearly 50 percent in Scenario B.

- China's GDP growth rate in Scenario A over the 2000–2015 period is slightly over 5 percent per annum, while in Scenario B the annual growth rate is below 3 percent.

- By 2015, China's GDP in Scenario A is more than three times that of Japan in PPP terms, but only 36 percent of Japan's GDP if nominal exchange rates are used for the dollar conversions. In Scenario B, the China GDP forecasts are more than 30 percent *below* those in Scenario A, both in PPP and XR terms.

- China's per-capita GDP nearly doubles between 2000 and 2015 in PPP terms but still remains well below $10 thousand in 2015 in Scenario A.

- China's military spending and military capital rise substantially in Scenario A, as a consequence of forecasted GDP growth and posited military investment, respectively. By 2015, China's military capital is more than four times that of Japan in terms of the purchasing power of the yuan for investment goods (PI) and is about the same as Japan's in terms of nominal exchange rates. In Scenario B, China's military spending and military capital are, respectively, 45 percent and 30 percent below those in Scenario A.

INDIA

When the Bharatiya Janata Party (BJP) came to power in 1996, its election platform contained three goals relevant for our forecasts: (1) further liberalization of the economy, (2) limiting the role of foreign multinational corporations, and (3) making India an overt nuclear power. These goals remain useful guideposts for forecasting India's economic and military future because a broad consensus underlies each of them, and this consensus has been strengthened by the BJP's reelection in 1999. For example, most Indian policymakers agree on the need to retreat from the regulatory excesses of previous decades. Similarly, for historical and political reasons, most policymakers are ambivalent toward foreign corporations and investors, both courting and resisting them. Finally, having decided to display and enhance India's overt nuclear capability, policymakers are expected to turn to the design of appropriate doctrines to guide and control its use.

In the present analysis, we have considered two different scenarios: a conservative-growth case, and a feasible high-growth forecast. We report here only the conservative-growth scenario. The high-growth scenario registers about one percentage point higher annual GDP growth than the conservative case, with correspondingly enhanced effects on military spending and military capital growth. The conservative forecast is constructed from the same assumptions adopted in our earlier work.[13] These assumptions are largely internal to the Indian economy, eschewing any heroic role for either foreign investment or exports, or heroic reform of the public sector, in keeping with how the Indian economy has been managed during the past two decades.

The "feasible" high-growth scenario is designed to capture the effect of aggressive action that might be taken on at least two additional fronts: raising the share of GDP devoted to investment and attracting greater levels of foreign-portfolio and foreign-direct investment. The former goal is difficult to achieve without terminating public-sector dissaving, either through efficiency improvements or through divestiture. The high-growth scenario should be interpreted as a statement about India's economic potential that can be realized through aggressive policy reform without incurring unacceptable political risks; it should not be interpreted as a statement about India's "maximum" economic potential, which could be even greater.

The high-growth scenario is based upon the following three key assumptions. First, the ratio of GDP devoted to investment is assumed to increase from approximately 25 percent in 1998 to 30 percent in 2005 and remain at that level thereafter. Second, foreign-direct and -portfolio investment will rise gradually from $5 billion per year in 1993 to a modest $15 billion (in 1998 U.S. dollars) by 2005, and stay at that level. The effect of foreign investment decreases proportionally in later years as the Indian economy grows in size. Third, Indian policymakers are assumed to channel foreign investment strategically so as to acquire new technology, boosting TFP to 2 percent per year from 2005 onward, compared with 1.5 percent between 1998 and 2005.

That the Indian economy can grow faster than our conservative forecast is amply borne out by the economy's actual performance between 1993 and 1997 (that is, post–economic reform and pre–Southeast Asia crisis). During this period, Indian GDP grew at an annual compound rate of 7.2 percent, compared with our earlier forecast of 5.8 percent. Several factors account for this discrepancy: (1) a postreform, short-term spurt in economic efficiency over and above

---

[13]See Wolf et al., 1995, pp. 49–52.

our long-term TFP estimate; (2) back-to-back favorable monsoon years leading to healthy agricultural growth; (3) improved export performance; and (4) increasing foreign-direct and -portfolio investment (3–5 billion U.S. dollars per year since 1993.[14] As a point of reference, China attracts roughly 30–40 billion U.S. dollars per year of direct and portfolio investment.

However, the impressive economic performance of the 1993–1997 period will be difficult to sustain. Favorable monsoons cannot occur repeatedly, and the East Asian financial crisis has caused Indian exports to lose some of their growth. Because of these factors, future economic growth rates are more likely to approach our earlier forecast of 5.5 percent per year on average for the 2000–2015 period. These rates are reflected in the conservative forecasts shown in Table 9. If Indian policymakers were to aggressively reform the public sector and pursue greater levels of foreign investment, as their public statements indicate, then a higher annual growth rate of 6.6 percent is clearly attainable.

The forecasts of India's economic and military trends (in terms of both XR and PPP conversion rates) from 1995 to 2015 are summarized in Table 9.

Nevertheless, the conservative-growth scenario results in forecasts that are 60–70 percent above those made in our earlier work.[15] These higher estimates are a result of the following factors:

- India's GDP growth in the 1994–1999 period was considerably higher than was previously forecast.

- The purchasing-power-parity value of the rupee has risen relative to the dollar (that is to say, domestic prices are lower relative to world market prices) than in the earlier Penn World Tables estimates, thereby boosting Indian aggregates in dollar terms.

It is also worth noting that India's national accounts may soon be revised to capture more fully income generated in the informal sec-

---

[14]M. Brahmbhatt, T. G. Srinivasan, and K. Murrell, *India in the Global Economy*, Washington, D.C.: World Bank, 1996.

[15]See Wolf et al., 1995, pp. 49–52.

Table 9

India Trends, 1995–2015

	1995	2000	2005	2010	2015
GDP (billions of 98$)					
XR	359	481	636	833	1,073
PPP	2,227	2,990	3,952	5,174	6,666
Average annual growth rate (%)		5.43	6.07	5.73	5.54
Per-capita GDP (thousands of 98$)					
XR	0.4	0.5	0.6	0.7	0.8
PPP	2.4	2.9	3.5	4.3	5.1
Military spending (billions of 98$)					
XR	10.3	16.8	25.4	33.3	42.9
PPP	64.1	105	158.1	207	267
Military capital (billions of 98$)					
XR	29	32.2	43.8	60.5	81.3
PI	112	124.2	169.1	233.6	314

NOTES: See Appendix B; parameters: $\tau = 1.5\%/\text{yr}$, $\alpha = 0.55$, $\gamma = 4\%$, $\pi = 25\%$, $\delta = 8-10\%/\text{yr}$, LdotL = 2.2%/yr, KdotK = 5.7%/yr.

tor of the economy, and this correction is likely to raise GDP estimates by more than 10 percent.[16]

In our forecasts of India's military spending in the 2000–2015 period, we estimate that the military spending share of GDP is 4 percent, which is slightly higher than the officially reported figures. However, the official statistics are generally thought to understate total defense spending. In particular, the official statistics on military spending evidently do not include the military components of the National Space and Nuclear programs which, though modest in the past, will probably increase in the future. If appropriate allowance is made to include India's current and prospectively increased outlays for nu-

---

[16]E. Lane, *Dow Jones Newswires*, March 23, 1999.

clear weapons and delivery systems, we believe the 4 percent military spending share of GDP is quite conservative.[17]

In estimating India's military capital stock, we assume that 25 percent of the defense budget is devoted to military investment in the 2000–2015 period, which is the approximate figure devoted to military investment in the 1990s.

In constructing the time series forecast for India's military capital stock, the same procedure is followed as with the other countries: New military investment is added to the previously accumulated stock in each successive year, while the military capital stock as of 1994 is depreciated at a 10 percent annual rate, and military investments made after 1994 are depreciated at 8 percent.

As Table 9 and Figures 13–16 indicate, India's GDP more than doubles between 2000 and 2015, reaching $6.7 trillion in PPP 1998 U.S. dollars, representing about 54 percent of China's GDP—about 5 percent greater than its present GDP relative to China's.

Per-capita GDP in India reaches 5.1 thousand PPP U.S. 1998 dollars, about 60 percent of China's.

In PPP terms, military spending increases more than two-and-one-half times from the present level by 2015 ($267 billion in 2015, compared with $105 billion in 2000).

By 2015, India's military capital stock reaches $314 billion in PI terms, about 62 percent of China's military capital ($666 billion), compared with only 48 percent of China's military capital stock in the year 2000.

It should be noted that all of these comparisons are based on the conservative-growth scenario for India and the sustained-growth

---

[17]Based upon detailed analysis of India's defense budget in the early 1990s, S. Gordon has suggested that official defense spending estimates should be increased by 20 percent to allow for defense-related spending by public-sector enterprises. See S. Gordon, *India's Rise to Power,* New York, 1995; and S. Gordon, "Indian Defense Spending: Treading Water in the Fiscal Deep," *Asian Survey #10,* 1992.

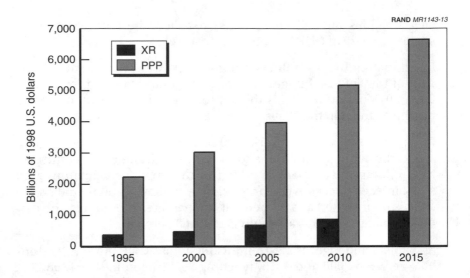

Figure 13—India Trends, 1995–2015: GDP

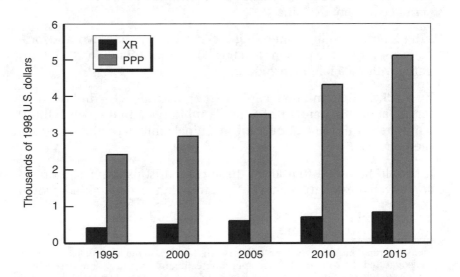

Figure 14—India Trends, 1995–2015: GDP Per Capita

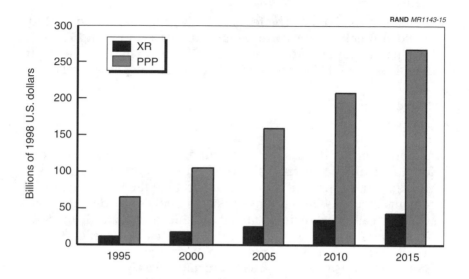

Figure 15—India Trends, 1995–2015: Military Spending

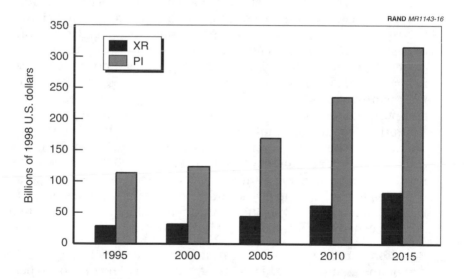

Figure 16—India Trends, 1995–2015: Military Capital

Scenario A for China. The feasible high-growth scenario for India would further boost the corresponding forecasts by about 15 percent. If China's disrupted-growth Scenario (B) were to materialize, the Indian figures would be raised further, by about 30 percent relative to China's.

KOREA

As noted earlier, the assumptions underlying our present forecasts for Korea differ substantially from those adopted in the earlier work.[18] For our present forecasts, we assume the Korean peninsula remains divided. Our current estimates apply only to South Korea, while the earlier estimates assumed reunification of North and South Korea under the aegis of the South. As discussed earlier, by 1999 South Korea began but did not complete its recovery from the sharp economic reversals of 1997–1998, returning to a significantly positive (over 5 percent) GDP growth rate in 1999, although still well below the rates prior to 1997.

Our earlier RAND forecasts also erred in failing to anticipate the 1997 plunge in asset and currency values, resulting in a deep reversal from GDP growth rates of 9–10 percent per annum to a negative rate of 4 percent in 1998. Consequently, caution is warranted in assessing our current forecasts. Although the South Korean economic picture remains mixed, the signs of recovery are distinctly positive. South Korea's reform efforts have involved substantial opening to both direct and portfolio investment from abroad, significant improvement in the term structure of South Korea's large foreign debt, and the buildup of large foreign exchange reserves (about $60 billion), as a result of current account surpluses in 1998 and 1999. However, the process of restructuring South Korea's *chaebol*-dominated industry—the *chaebol* are the large, multisector conglomerates, such as Daewoo, Samsung, and Hyundai—and reforming its banking system has proceeded slowly and only to a limited degree.

Based on data analysis over the past several decades through 1997, and on the assumption of a labor share in national income of 60 percent (the parameter α in the model described in Appendix A), we

---

[18]See Wolf et al., pp. 45–49.

have estimated long-term growth in total factor productivity (the parameter τ) of 3 percent annually. We assume further that the labor and capital inputs grow annually by 0.5–1.0 percent and between 0.2 and 7.1 percent, respectively. These assumptions are based on labor force projections from the International Labor Organization.[19]

The extraordinarily wide range in the growth of capital results from several considerations: First, the International Monetary Fund's data on Korea's annual investments imply a decline in the capital stock (because depreciation exceeds new investment). Second, over the forecast period, we assume investment is sufficient to raise the annual growth of capital to a "long-run" growth rate of slightly more than 7 percent, a figure that is at the lower end of Korea's historical range during 1975–1997, which is reasonable for the forecast period. The GDP growth rate that results for the period 2000–2015 is slightly above 5 percent, substantially below the 7.9 percent growth rate estimated in our 1995 study. This decline from the earlier estimate is attributable to the reduction in estimated total factor productivity growth, the effect of the 1997–1998 recession in reducing the level of GDP in the early years of the forecast period, and the effect of the recession on new investment and thus upon Korean civilian capital stock.

Our projections indicate that Korea's GDP and per-capita GDP more than double between 2000 and 2015 (see Table 10 and Figures 17–20).[20] Korea's military spending is also projected to increase substantially between 2000 and 2015, although the rate of this increase and the absolute amount of the increase (from $24.7 billion in 2000 in 1998 PPP dollars to $53.9 billion in 2015) are below the corresponding estimates in our 1995 analysis.[21]

---

[19]See Appendix B and International Labor Office, 1997 and 1996, interpolated.

[20]This projected doubling in per-capita GDP is similar to the projection in our earlier work, except that the dollar values in the current projections are significantly above those in the earlier work. The principal reasons for this are that the present projections are for South Korea alone while the earlier ones included the North (which had a depressing effect on the absolute level of per-capita GDP), the use of more recent PPP conversion rates, and the expression of the current results in 1998 dollars, versus 1994 dollars in the earlier work.

[21]However, it should be noted that this rate of increase as well as the level at which it ensues are substantially (20–30 percent) below those projected in our earlier work.

Table 10

Korea Trends, 1995–2015

	1995	2000	2005	2010	2015
GDP (billions of 98$)					
XR[a]	306	344	418	565	774
PPP	663	744	905	1223	1676
Average annual					
growth rate (%)	2.3	4	6.2	6.5	
Per-capita GDP (thousands of 98$)					
XR	6.8	7.3	8.6	11.3	15.1
PPP	14.7	15.9	18.6	24.4	32.8
Military spending (billions of 98$)					
XR	10.1	11.4	13.5	18.2	24.9
PPP	21.9	24.7	29.1	39.3	53.9
Military capital (billions of 98$)					
XR	25.4	30.8	35.3	43.5	56.9
PI	55	61.4	70.4	86.8	113.5

[a]End of 1998 XR = 1204 won/$.

NOTES: See Appendix B; parameters: $\tau = 3\%/\text{yr}$, $\alpha = 0.6\%$, $\gamma = 3.5\%$, $\pi = 30\%$, $\delta = 8$–$10\%/\text{yr}$, LdotL = 0.5–1.0%/yr, KdotK = –(0.2) to +(7.1)%/yr.

As Table 10 indicates, Korea's military capital stock is projected to increase by 85 percent from 2000 to 2015 in 1998 dollars, using the PPP for investment goods to convert from won to dollars (from $61.4 billion in 2000 to $113.5 billion in 2015). Thus, by 2015, Korea's military capital would be approximately equal to that of Japan, while Korea's current military capital stock is less than 60 percent of Japan's. Furthermore, South Korea's GDP would rise during this 15-year period from about one-quarter of Japan's GDP in 2000 to nearly one-half of it by 2015 (in PPP dollars).

Again, the explanation lies in the fact that the earlier estimates included military spending for a reunified North and South Korea. See Wolf et al., 1995, p. 48.

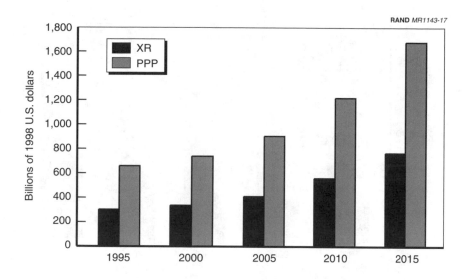

Figure 17—Korea Trends, 1995–2015: GDP

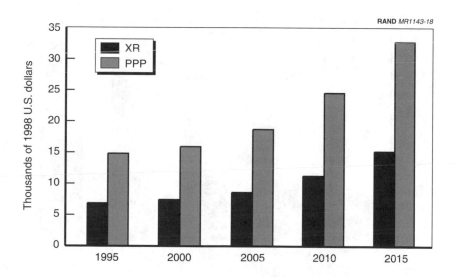

Figure 18—Korea Trends, 1995–2015: GDP Per Capita

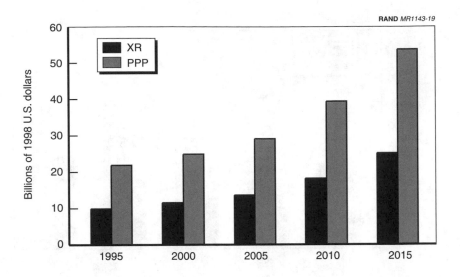

Figure 19—Korea Trends, 1995–2015: Military Spending

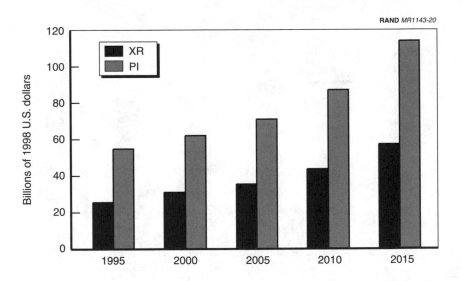

Figure 20—Korea Trends, 1995–2015: Military Capital

INDONESIA

The greatest uncertainty in our forecasts for the five countries involves Indonesia. Despite generally successful completion of its June 1999 elections for the Indonesian National Assembly and the December presidential election, the country's political outlook remains cloudy and is still further obscured by the turmoil in East Timor and Aceh. Tensions between Indonesia's political and military leadership are acute, and the outlook for stable political leadership remains dubious at the end of 1999.

In this situation, the role of Indonesia's military establishment—sometimes a force for internal stability—is also highly uncertain, as are the resulting effects on military spending and new military investment in Indonesia.

Nevertheless, there have been some limited signs of improvement in the Indonesian economy. The GDP seems to have ended its sharp decline, and in 1999 the rupiah recovered about half its deep depreciation from the two preceding years. Inflation has cooled, and Indonesia's international payments are less adverse than during the two preceding years. However, banking reform, bankruptcy legislation, and other institutional reforms have been delayed. Consequently, our projections should be treated with even greater reservations and caution than are warranted for the other four economies dealt with in this analysis.

Table 11 summarizes Indonesia's GDP, per-capita GDP, military spending, and military capital investments for the period from 1995 through 2015. Because of both the sharp economic reversals experienced in 1997–1999 and the continuing instability in the economy and polity, the forecasts summarized in Table 11 project GDP growth rates 15–30 percent below those forecast in RAND's prior work.[22]

---

[22]Unpublished RAND research by Charles Wolf, Jr., and Michael Kennedy on long-term economic and military trends in Russia, Germany, and Indonesia.

Table 11

Indonesia Trends, 1995–2015

	1995	2000	2005	2010	2015
GDP (billions of 98$)					
XR	59	62	75	92	114
PPP	722	748	908	1123	1390
Average annual growth rate (%)	0.01	3.9	4.4	4.4	
Per-capita GDP (thousands of 98$)					
XR	0.3	0.3	0.3	0.4	0.5
PPP	3.7	3.5	4.0	4.7	5.5
Military spending (billions of 98$)					
XR	1.1	1.1	1.5	1.8	2.3
PPP	13	13.5	18.1	22.5	27.8
Military capital (billions of 98$)					
XR	5	4.1	4	4.3	5
PI	46.6	38.9	37.3	40.6	47.3

NOTES: See Appendix B; parameters: $\tau = 1.9\%/yr$, $\alpha = 0.6$, $\gamma = 1.8–2\%$, $\pi = 25\%$, $\delta = 8–10\%/yr$, LdotL = 1–2.5%/yr, KdotK = 2–7.2%/yr.

Although all the forecasts reported in the present study show a substantial difference between the dollar estimates based on nominal exchange rates and on real purchasing-power-parity rates, in the Indonesian case the difference between the two estimates is more than an order of magnitude—by far the highest discrepancy among the five countries. The reason for this enormous difference lies in the extent of depreciation of the Indonesian rupiah, by 80 percent over the period preceding and following the mid-1997 financial crisis. Consequently, the nominal exchange rate estimates in Table 11 are misleadingly low. However, the PPP-adjusted rate may imply an overvaluation of the rupiah because of internal price inflation triggered by the sharp currency devaluation, but not reflected in the Penn World Tables data through 1995.

A more accurate picture of the Indonesian economy might be conveyed by averaging the PPP and nominal exchange rate estimates shown in Table 11, a procedure we forgo in the interests of avoiding further complications. Nevertheless, several points can be high-lighted from the Table 11 estimates:

- Indonesia's real GDP will probably regain its 1995 level by 2005.

- Military spending in 2015 in PPP terms will be about half that of Korea's.

- Although military capital, as estimated from the PPP index for in-vestment goods, rises slightly over the period from 2000 to 2015, it falls appreciably relative to the military capital stock of other countries in the region.

SENSITIVITY TESTS

We have performed limited sensitivity testing of the key parameters according to the following procedure: first, raising and lowering the parameter values by plus-or-minus one-half of the standard devia-tions of their respective historic means; second, inserting these changed values separately, one at a time, in the model to determine their effects on the resulting forecasts; and third, repeating the sec-ond step, but with all of the altered parameter values inserted simul-taneously rather than separately—that is, all parameters were in-creased or decreased by one-half of the standard deviations from their historic means.

In general, the sensitivity of the forecasts varies among the five coun-tries and among the several parameters in expected ways. If the standard deviation of a particular parameter in a particular country is large relative to that of the same parameter in another country, the resulting effect on GDP, military spending, and military capital will be greater. Among the several parameters, variations in the factor productivity parameter, τ, has the largest effect on the forecasts. Un-surprisingly, changing all of the parameter values simultaneously— whether up or down—alters the forecasts much more than the sepa-rate, one-at-a-time changes.

For example, for Japan an increase of one-half of the standard devia-tion in the capital growth parameter, KdotK, would raise forecasted GDP in 2015 by 8.8 percent (from 6.8 trillion to 7.4 trillion in 1998 dollars). A similar but separate increase in the employment growth parameter, LdotL, and in the factor productivity parameter, τ, would raise GDP in 2015 by 9 percent and 12.9 percent, respectively. The same three parameter changes would have the effect of raising forecasted military spending in 2015 by 8 percent, 3 percent, and 13 percent, respectively. When all of the parameters are simultaneously raised by one-half of the standard deviations from their historic means, the effects are understandably magnified: GDP and military spending in 2015 would thereby increase by 27 percent and 29 percent, respectively. It should be evident, however, that the likelihood of all parameters changing simultaneously in the same direction, rather than separately and perhaps in offsetting directions, is remote.

For China, the sensitivity of results to parameter changes is much greater because the corresponding standard deviations from the parameters' historic means are larger. Thus, separately increasing the capital growth, employment growth, and factor productivity growth parameters by one-half the standard deviations from their historic means would raise GDP in 2015 (for China's stable growth Scenario A) by 30 percent, 25 percent, and 55 percent, respectively. Correspondingly, military spending in 2015 would increase by 27 percent, 23 percent, and 53 percent, respectively (assuming that military spending is 2 percent of China's GDP). Again, when all parameter values are simultaneously raised, the effects on GDP and military spending are greatly magnified: GDP and military spending increase by 62 percent and 45 percent, respectively.

It should be noted that reductions in the parameter values by one-half of the corresponding standard deviations have generally symmetric effects to those above, but in a downward direction.

DECOMPOSITION OF INVESTMENT

To further test the plausibility of our modeling assumptions, we have examined the supportability of capital stock growth rates. The situation differs for each of the five countries.

- In Japan, the value of the capital growth parameter posited in our forecasts decreases over the 15-year period from 5 percent per year in the 2000–2005 period, to 4 percent per year in 2005–2010, to 3 percent per year in 2010–2015, for reasons discussed in the text. The annual GDP growth rate during the corresponding periods rises from 0.92 percent, to 1.56 percent, to 1.62 percent, respectively. The effect of these trends is to raise the implied investment share of GDP from 13 percent in 2000, to 16 percent in 2005, to 18 percent in 2010, and 19 percent in 2015. While the 6 percent increase over the 15 years is substantial, it is important to realize that Japan's current account surplus is now about 5 percent of its GDP. So, Japan's domestic savings rate, which includes both the current account surplus and domestic investment, is already sufficient to finance this scale of increase in the investment rate. A decline in and eventual elimination of Japan's current account surplus would make our forecasts entirely reasonable, even without drawing down of Japan's FX reserves which, at about $225 billion, are the world's largest. Furthermore, Japan's savings rates in the 1970s and 1980s were more than the 19 percent rate referred to above, so precedents for higher rates already exist.

The capital growth figures used for Japan are based on data from the *Japan Statistical Yearbook,* 1998. Annual capital growth as measured therein is defined this way: The "gross capital stock as of the end of each year (or each quarter) after 1970 is estimated on the basis of the value of assets made available by the 1955 and 1970 'National Wealth Survey,' by adding to or subtracting from it annual investments or asset removals made since. The assets covered are limited to reproducible tangible fixed assets, excluding private non-profit entities. Dwelling houses which do not serve directly as a means of production are also excluded from the coverage."

Some growth models do and others do not include residential housing. The ones that exclude it do so because of variability and noncomparability of data on residential investment, difficulties in imputing housing services to housing investment, difficulties in appraising the value of the housing stock, etc.

What matters for our estimates is that what's done is done consistently. In the Japan estimates, residential housing is excluded from the capital stock in the base period (i.e., the Japan Statistical Bureau does not provide a separate estimate of the housing stock), so residential investment was correspondingly excluded from the annual capital growth estimates. If it were to be included in the latter, this would amount to raising the investment shares of GDP by approximately 5–6 percent.

- In China, the capital growth parameter is assumed to decrease from 8 percent per year at the beginning of the 2000–2015 period to 4 percent per year by the end of the period, while annual GDP growth is rising from 4.9 percent to 5.3 percent (NB: The increase in GDP growth is due to the assumption of an increase in factor productivity growth from 1 percent at the start of the period to 1.5 percent during the last five years of the period, for reasons relating to the progress of reform and other reasons discussed in the text). During the 15-year period covered by the forecasts, the investment rate implied by the capital growth parameter is assumed to be equal to the annual savings rate, rising with the latter from 25 percent in 2000 to 30 percent in 2015. These rates are at or below current and recent savings rates in China, so the prospect of financing the assumed capital growth figures appears to be quite reasonable even without capital inflows. This, of course, is not intended to imply that capital inflows will not occur, or that they are not desirable on several other grounds.

- In India, the issue of an increasing investment rate does not arise because the rate of GDP growth projected in our estimates is actually slightly above the rate of capital growth: Annual GDP growth over the 15-year period is 5.8 percent, while annual capital growth is 5.7 percent. The investment share of GDP remains pegged at 25 percent throughout the period in the "conservative" scenario reported in our study. This rate is about equal to India's savings rates in recent years (i.e., capital inflows have been quite small), so there is no apparent problem of investment financing over the period we cover in our estimates.

- In Korea, the annual rate of capital growth rises substantially from near-zero at the start of the forecast period in 2000, to 7 percent by the end of the period in 2015. Annual GDP growth averages 5.6 percent over the 15 years, starting at 4 percent per year in the first five years, and reaching 6.5 percent during the final five years. The investment share of GDP implied by these calculations rises from an annual rate of 18.1 percent in 2000 to 29.6 percent in 2015. While this is a substantial increase, it has ample precedent in Korea's annual savings rates in the 1980s and 1990s, which averaged 29 percent and 35 percent, respectively. So, financing of the implied investment rates does not appear to be a problem. Once again, this does not imply that capital inflows are not now, nor will not be in the future, desirable on other grounds besides financing capital growth.

- In Indonesia, capital growth also rises substantially from an annual rate of 2 percent in 2000, to 7.2 percent by the end of the period covered by our estimates. Over the same 15 years, GDP grows at a rate of 4 percent at the start of the period to a rate of 6.5 percent in the final five years (2010–2015). The investment share of GDP correspondingly rises from 22 percent in 2000 to 32.8 percent, plainly a big increase. Nevertheless, the problem of financing this increase from a combination of domestic savings and capital inflows does not appear to be insuperable: In the 1980s and 1990s, Indonesia's savings rates averaged above 30 percent.

The conclusion from this is that the problem of financing the investment rates implied by these forecasts appears to be manageable in each of the five countries, although it will be more difficult in some (e.g., Indonesia) than in others (e.g., China and Japan).

Chapter Five

LINKING THE SEPARATE FORECASTS: REGIONAL INDEXING AND FUTURE SECURITY ENVIRONMENTS

In describing the methodology used in our forecasts, we noted the flaw involved in neglecting possible interactions among the five countries. Paradoxically, our forecasts might turn out to err because of feedback effects of forecasts that were initially accurate. For example, Japan's military spending and military investment might increase above the magnitudes indicated by our forecasts if rapid progress occurred in military modernization in China and Korea. Either of these developments, and *a fortiori* their joint occurrence, could have significant effects on Japan, thereby invalidating our forecasts for Japan. Thus, our estimates, or at least some of them, might turn out to be "self-preventing" (or "self-correcting"), in contrast to "self-fulfilling" forecasts.[1]

Despite this inherent shortcoming, use of the same methodology in previous RAND work resulted in prescient forecasts. The prior work produced forecasts of economic and military trends in Japan, Russia (then the Soviet Union), and Germany for the 1990s that were reasonably accurate, as well as contrary to the consensus prevailing when these earlier estimates were made.[2] However, we acknowledge that our previous work did not anticipate the financial crisis in East

---

[1]See the discussion of "self-preventing" versus "self-fulfilling" forecasts, Wolf et al., 1995, pp. 19–20.

[2]Wolf et al., 1995; Wolf et al., 1989; and unpublished RAND research by Gregory Hildebrandt, Joseph Nation, et al., on economic and military trends through 2010 in Germany, Japan, and the U.S.S.R.

Asia in the 1997–1998 period, nor the continued division between South and North Korea.

Quite apart from the problems presented by possible interactions among the five countries, another question arises: How can the separate country estimates be related to and associated with one other, so as to draw inferences concerning security issues in the region?

Two approaches to answering this question are adopted in this chapter: regional indexing and the formulation of alternative future security environments in the Asian region.

REGIONAL INDEXING

One way of assessing the security-related balance of forces implied by our forecasts is to focus on the GDPs and military capital stocks as crude, aggregate indicators of economic and military power, respectively, among the five countries. It is self-evident that each of these measures conveys only partial and limited elements of the corresponding dimensions of national power.

GDP provides a very broad measure of an economy's total output. It says nothing about the net resources above essential consumption requirements that an economy disposes of, nor about the capacity of fiscal and other institutions to mobilize these resources to further national purposes. GDP does not convey anything about the technological and skill capabilities that are nested within this aggregate measure, nor about environmental damage or other nonmonetized public injuries that an economy may be incurring.

In an analogous sense, a country's aggregate stock of military capital (i.e., its holdings of military equipment, communications, bases, and supporting facilities) conveys only a very limited measure of military capabilities. These depend to an equal or greater extent on other factors, including human, organizational, and technical ones. The human and organizational factors that military capital does not embrace include the leadership, training, morale, and skills of its armed forces. The excluded technical factors encompass command, control, communications, and intelligence functions, as well as logistic support capabilities. And, of course, military capital conveys nothing about the regional alliances or adversarial circumstances that may respectively enhance or diminish a country's military capabilities.

Granted these limitations, GDP and military capital have some utility in conveying a sense of the changes in the relative balance of forces implied by our forecasts.

Toward this end, Tables 12 and 13 and Figures 21 and 22 present indexes of the GDPs and military capital stocks of Japan, China, India, Korea, and Indonesia between 2000 and 2015, reflecting the forecasts summarized in preceding chapters. The respective indexes use our estimates for Korea in 2000 as the regional numeraire, scaling the other four countries to this base.

Tables 12 and 13 and Figures 21 and 22 are based on PPP conversion rates for GDP, and the PI rate for military capital, to convert constant-price time-series data in local currencies into 1998 U.S. dollars.

Several points emerge from these regional indexes:

- Japan's relative economic and military power in the region diminishes appreciably from 2000 to 2015, vis-à-vis both China and Korea.

- Consequently, the value that Japan will place on its security alliance with the United States is likely to rise, and/or Japanese efforts to reform and liberalize its economy, and to enhance its independent military capabilities while attenuating its alliance connections, might ensue.

- China's economic and military power diminishes somewhat relative to that of India. However, the absolute gap between the levels of China's GDP and military capital, on the one hand, and those of the other principal countries, on the other, grows substantially. The point highlights the importance of the U.S. role in the region's security balance.

- Indonesia's relative and absolute stature in the region recedes.

Table 12

Linking the Forecasts: Indexing GDPs

	2000	2015	
GDP (PPP)[a]			
Korea	100	225	(100)
Japan	395	488	(217)
China	804	1,672	(742)
India	402	896	(398)
Indonesia	101	187	(83)

[a]Indexed on Korea's GDP in 2000, forecasted at $744 billion in PPP 1998 U.S. dollars; forecasted to rise 225 percent by 2015 to $1.6 trillion. Figures in parentheses are indexed on Korea's GDP in 2015.

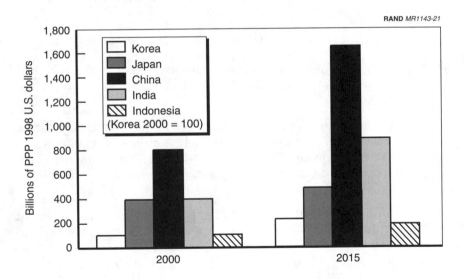

Figure 21—Linking the Forecasts: Indexing GDPs

Table 13

Linking the Forecasts: Indexing Military Capital

	2000	2015	
Military capital (PI)[a]			
Korea	100	185	(100)
Japan	187	194	(205)
China	393–450	799–1,033	(421–559)
India	204	514	(277)
Indonesia	63	77	(42)

[a]Indexed on Korea's military capital in 2000, forecasted at $61 billion in PI 1998 U.S. dollars; forecasted to rise 185 percent by 2015 to $113.5 billion. Figures in parentheses are indexed on Korea's military capital in 2015.

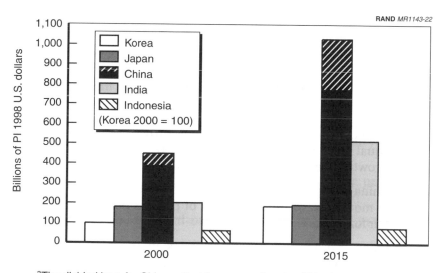

[a]The divided bars for China reflect the assumption that China's annual military spending may vary between 2 percent and 3 percent of GDP.

Figure 22—Linking the Forecasts: Indexing Military Capital

longer run, resources for military modernization and preparedness may grow, as a result of general wariness and cautionary concerns combined with easing of economic constraints on military spending.

PROSPECTS FOR MULTILATERAL SECURITY COOPERATION

Multilateral institutions in the Asian region, including but not confined to those concerned with security matters, have an informal, consensual, and somewhat academic character, rather than a formal actionable one. This characterization reflects many distinguishing factors about the region—including its enormous diversity in size, national interests, national histories and traditions, and economic structures—in comparison especially with Europe, as well as Latin America. Even the two longest-standing multilateral institutions in the region—the Asia Pacific Economic Cooperation Forum (APEC) and ASEAN, which generally focus on economic rather than security matters—function as discussion forums, rather than as action-oriented bodies.[3]

In the security domain, the principal multilateral organizations are the ASEAN Regional Forum (ARF), the Council on Security Cooperation in the Asia Pacific (CSCAP) and the Track-Two Dialogues. The latter two groups consist mainly of academic and other nongovernment organizations. ARF, which represents governments and is typically led by the foreign ministers of the participating members, is intended to provide a forum for discussing security issues throughout the Asian region, extending from India in the west to Korea and Russia in the northeast, and including the United States as well as China and Japan.

One of ARF's limitations arises from the fact that, as an offshoot of ASEAN, its organization and agenda are vested in the Southeast Asian members of ASEAN. Some of the Southeast Asian countries have begun to consider the possibility of enhancing ARF's stature by having the chairing of its meetings, as well as the organization of its

---

[3]For a useful summary of these institutions, see Douglas Paal, *Nesting the Alliances in the Emerging Context of Asia-Pacific Multilateral Processes: A U.S. Perspective,* July 1999, Stanford, Calif.: The Asia Pacific Research Center, Stanford University.

secretariat and agenda, rotate among other members outside of ASEAN itself.

Nevertheless, there are several reasons why the economic problems still besetting the Asian region are likely to impede prospects for ARF and other groups concerned with multilateral security cooperation in the region, at least in the short to medium term. First, political leaders in Asia, and the resources at their disposal, are focusing their attention on their economic challenges and the means of surmounting them, with less attention and fewer resources devoted to regional security activities. Second, there is some evidence of increased fractiousness in the region, often not tied to the economic and financial turmoil, but perhaps exacerbated by it. Examples include territorial disputes between Malaysia and Singapore, disputes over sovereignty and oil and gas exploitation in the South China Sea involving the Spratly Islands, and the generally rogue behavior of North Korea.

At the same time, it is plausible that security cooperation between the two U.S. alliance structures—with Japan and with Korea—may be enhanced as a side effect of the region's economic turmoil. Quite apart from potential security contingencies in Asia—especially in Taiwan and on the Korean peninsula—the three alliance participants have the added motivation to increase their security cooperation so as to save resources, and/or increase the efficiency of their use. This may lead to further efforts toward interoperability in operations and maintenance; improved coordination in command, control, communications, and intelligence; and perhaps joint systems development and acquisition including TMD (theater missile defense) and other systems.

BURDEN SHARING

In considering burden-sharing issues in light of the Asian economic adversities, there are important reasons why substantial shares should be borne by America's allies. These reasons are both economic and political—economic from the standpoint of easing the preponderant resource burden shouldered by the United States, and political from the standpoint of reflecting and substantiating the joint nature of the alliances.

Bearing this in mind, how should burden sharing in Asia be viewed in light of altered economic circumstances in Japan and Korea?

Japan's sharing of in-country costs has been by far the largest of any U.S. ally's contribution, and Korea's sharing remains substantial. Figure 23 shows the comparative burden-sharing outlays of Japan and Korea, compared with those of NATO members.

As Figure 23 indicates, about 75 percent of in-country costs other than military salaries for U.S. forces have been borne by Japan, compared with over 64 percent in the case of Korea. These high proportions of shared burdens contrast sharply with only 30 to 40 percent shares in the NATO countries shown. Notwithstanding the serious structural problems besetting the Japanese economy, as discussed in Chapter Two, there is no convincing economic reason why Japan's cost-sharing burden should be reduced, especially in light of Japan's

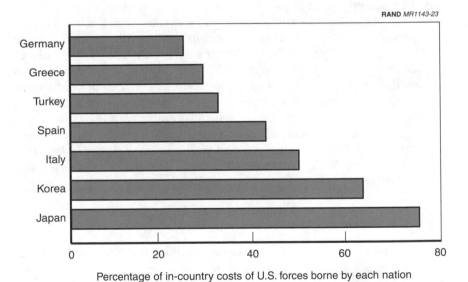

Percentage of in-country costs of U.S. forces borne by each nation

SOURCE: Adapted from *Report on Allied Contributions to the Common Defense*, 1997.

Figure 23—Burden Sharing of Japan and Korea Compared with NATO Countries

huge foreign exchange reserves. Were the United States to defray with dollar outlays a portion of Japan's burden sharing of in-country costs, the net effect would simply be to add to these foreign exchange reserves.

However, there might be a political reason for some modest reduction in Japan's burden sharing—as a testimonial by the United States to its alliance commitment with Japan. Although our forecasts for Japan's future growth envisage only very modest rates through 2015, there is no evident way in which a reduction of Japan's burden sharing of the joint alliance costs would contribute to higher GDP growth. Gradual changes in the structural rigidities of the Japanese economy would not in any discernible way be accelerated by reduced burden sharing.

The Korean case presents a different picture. As noted in earlier chapters, Korea has made considerable progress from its deep economic setbacks in 1997 and 1998, and our forecasts envisage resumption of medium growth rates in the coming years. Still, an economic argument can be made that a modest reduction in the substantial Korean share of in-country costs for U.S. Army forces could accelerate Korea's recovery by reducing some of the continued resource pressures on the economy. There may also be a political reason for such a modest adjustment—as an indication of U.S. recognition of Korea's problems as well as the U.S. commitment to its alliance with Korea.

In sum, in Japan there may be a political case for a reduction in burden sharing, while in Korea there may be both an economic and a political case for such an adjustment.

EFFECTS ON ATTITUDES TOWARD FORWARD-BASED U.S. FORCES

The main U.S. forward-based forces in Asia are in Korea and Japan, with U.S. Army forces predominating in Korea, and U.S. Navy forces predominating in Japan. The different economic problems in these two countries may have quite different effects in either providing support for or undermining the presence of U.S. forces.

METHOD AND MODEL

The forecasts of economic and military trends presented in this report are based on a hierarchically linked model in which (1) GDP (gross domestic product) or gross national product (GNP)[1] is estimated from a simple Cobb-Douglas production function, (2) percapita GDP is calculated using demographic data for each country in combination with the GDP estimates, (3) military spending is derived as a specified (sometimes varying) proportion of GDP, and (4) military capital stock is estimated as a specified (sometimes varying) proportion of military spending allocated to new military investment *minus* depreciation of the previously accumulated military capital stock.

Use of the CES (constant elasticity of substitution) model is based on its commendable transparency, convenience for calculation purposes, and its modest and tractable data requirements compared, say, with input-output models, translog production functions, or time-series regressions. The method used to derive military spending and military capital estimates was selected for similar reasons of tractability, simplicity, and transparency.

The model used in the forecasts consists of five variables (GDP, employed labor, nonmilitary capital, military spending, and military capital, each of which carries a time subscript) and seven parame-

---

[1]In most cases, the estimates we present are for GDP. In the case of India, the estimates are for GNP because the country data from which the estimates were made used GNP rather than GDP as a starting point. The accounting relation between GDP and GNP is defined as: GDP = GNP − net factor income from abroad.

ters—annual employment growth; annual growth of nonmilitary capital; total factor productivity (τ), representing the annual rate of technological change; the labor share in GDP (α); the proportion of GDP devoted to military spending (γ); the proportion of military spending devoted to military investment (π); and the annual depreciation rate (δ) of the previously accumulated military capital stock. The model is first applied to data covering the period from 1985 through 1996, and the parameters are estimated by calculating their mean values and variances over this period, and in some cases by a time regression of the parameter values in each year to determine trends.[2]

We then use these parameter values and appropriate values for the input variables based on the authors' explicit judgments about whether these trend values are likely to persist, or why they may be expected to change and by how much. These judgments are described and reflected in the individual country sections of Chapter Four.

The model summarized below was used for each country, together with adjustments and elaboration to allow for data problems or other country-specific circumstances.

$$Q = e^{\tau t} \cdot L^{\alpha} \cdot K^{(1-\alpha)} \tag{1}$$

$$MS_t = \gamma\, GDP \tag{2}$$

$$MK_t = \pi MS_t + MK_{t-1}(1-\delta) \tag{3}$$

In Equation (1):

Q   =   GDP

τ =   rate of technological change (total factor productivity)

t   =   years covered in the projections beginning with 1994

α =   labor share in GDP

---

[2]See Appendix B.

L   =   labor input in each year

K   =   capital input in each year.

In Equation (2):

MS_t =   military spending in year t

γ =   proportion of GDP devoted to military spending.

In Equation (3):

MK_t =   military capital stock in year t

π =   proportion of military spending devoted to procurement of equipment and construction

δ =   annual depreciation rate on the previously accumulated military capital stock.

In Equation (1), the civil capital inputs (K) and labor inputs (L), and their corresponding growth rates, were estimated for each country. The capital input, K, for each year was calculated by adding each year's net new investment to the previous year's civil capital stock. Note that this depreciation rate on the civil capital stock is not necessarily the same as the depreciation rate on the military capital stock.[3]

Equation (1) can be expressed in a form that is useful for our forecasts by taking the logarithmic derivatives of the variables with respect to time. The result is Equation (1a):

$$\dot{Q}/Q = \tau + \alpha\left(\dot{L}/L\right) + (1-\alpha)\left(\dot{K}/K\right) \tag{1a}$$

Equation (1a) stipulates that the rate of growth in GDP is equal to the annual growth of total factor productivity (technological progress) τ, plus the rate of growth in employment multiplied by the share of labor income in GDP (α), plus the rate of growth in the capital stock

---

[3]The initial year 1994 capital stock figures were derived from the Penn World Table (version 5.7) and an expanded set of international comparisons, 1950–1988 (see Robert Summers and Alan Heston, *The Quarterly Journal of Economics*, May 1991) and from the prior estimates in Wolf et al., 1989.

multiplied by the share of capital income in GDP, $(1 - \alpha)$. The rate of growth in total factor productivity in each country in recent years can be estimated from the known values of the other variables in Equation (1a).

The labor and capital income shares, (α) and $(1 - \alpha)$, respectively, are also based on the respective data and experience of each country.

Similarly, the estimates of the parameter γ, representing the share of GDP devoted to military spending, are calculated from each country's average share in recent years, combined with explicit judgments by the authors of this report, as noted above.

Measurement of the military capital stock presents complex and difficult theoretical and empirical problems. Among these difficulties are the following: First, the "services" provided by military equipment are difficult to define and quantify; second, the same piece of equipment can provide varying levels of effective service depending on the type of conflict, terrain, adversaries, allies, training, and morale of the forces, as well as various contingency-specific circumstances. Our methodology measures the value of the military capital stock based on procurement cost. This implicitly assumes that the value of military services provided by a particular piece of equipment or structure, relative to others, averaged over an appropriate set of scenarios, is equal to its procurement cost. This assumption is convenient, but arbitrary and untested.

A further difficulty in measuring military capital relates to the possibility of accelerated obsolescence depending on the technology embodied in an adversary's military capital and military forces.

Generally, in our analysis, the military capital stocks of the respective countries were calculated using constant-price outlays for military procurement and construction (covering barracks, airfields, communication facilities, and other structures). As with the civilian capital stock estimates referred to earlier, military capital estimates require that we have a benchmark estimate for at least a single year to enable the entire series to be generated. We have used various methods to establish the initial military capital stock figure, generally drawing on the estimates made in our earlier work.[4] We have assumed the same depreciation rate δ on military capital for each of the five countries, as described in the individual country sections of Chapter Four.[5]

It should be noted that our estimates for 1995 through 2015 assume that each country's military spending decisions are independent of those of other countries; i.e., reactive effects were not modeled.

---

[4]See Wolf et al., 1989.

[5]The annual depreciation rate, δ, has been arbitrarily set at 10 percent for military equipment acquired prior to 1994, and 8 percent for equipment procured thereafter.

PARAMETER VALUES: HISTORICAL PATTERNS AND STUDY ASSUMPTIONS

Table B.1 summarizes historical data on the means and standard deviations for the six principal parameters used in our forecasts.[1]

In choosing the periods from 1985 through 1996 as the reference decade for estimating means and standard deviations, we are deliberately setting aside the sharp economic reversals suffered in 1997 and 1998 by two of the five countries—Korea and Indonesia. Part of the reason for doing this is elaborated in the Chapter Two discussion of the end of the 1997–1998 financial crisis in East Asia. However, the gradual pace of recovery from the 1997–1998 East Asian crisis does affect judgments we make concerning several of the parameters for these countries, e.g., see footnotes e and f of Table B.1.

We use the historical data shown in Table B.1 as background for making explicit judgments about whether and why we believe the parameter values will change from their averages and the patterns of stability or volatility they displayed in the 1985–1996 period.

For example, the second row of Table B.1 for Japan (showing the parameter values assumed in this study) posits that employment and capital growth will be lower in Japan than their averages in the

---

[1]The six parameters do not include the same annual depreciation rate, δ, applied to the military capital stock of the five countries, as discussed in the text and in Appendix A.

Table B.1

Parameter Values: Historical Context and Current Assumptions

	Employment Growth $\dot{L}/L$ %/yr		Capital Growth $\dot{K}/K$, %/yr		Productivity Growth (τ), %/yr		Labor Share (α), %		Military Spending Share (γ), %		Military Investment Share (π), %	
	mean	S.D. (σ)	mean	S.D. (σ)	mean	S.D. (σ)	mean	S.D. (σ)	mean	S.D. (σ)	mean	S.D. (σ)
Japan												
1985–1996	1.05	.73	7.1	3.7	–0.35	1.71	63.7	2.5	1.01	.04	a	
Current assumption	0.3–04		3.0–5.0		–(1)+(0.4)		67.0		1.1		21	
China (Scenario A)												
1985–1997	2.18	0.76	37.9[b]	2.6	10.12[c]	3.29	61.17	3.35	1.46	0.34	d	
Current assumption	1–1.20		8–9.0		1.0–1.5		60.0		2.0–3.0		25–32	
India												
1986–1996	2.68	1.0	6.7	1.0	1.4–1.5	0.10			3.52	0.53	24.1	1.58
Current assumption	2.2		5.7		1.5		55.0		4.0		25	
Korea												
1985–1997	2.76	1.20	10.1	1.66	3.65	1.04	62.0	.08	3.25	0.03	30	0
Current assumption	0.5–1.0		–(0.2)+(7.1)[e]		3.0		60.0		3.5		30	
Indonesia												
1985–1997	2.71	2.27	3.99	0.80	1.91	1.01	60.3	.013	1.95	0.00	25	0.00
Current assumption	1.0–2.5		2.0–7.2[f]		1.9		60.0		1.8–2.0		25	

SOURCES: The principal sources for the historical data are as follows: Japan, *Statistical Yearbook, 1998*; China, *Statistical Yearbook, 1998*; India, M. Brahmbhatt, T. G. Srinivasan, K. Murrell, *India in the Global Economy*, World Bank, 1996; I. J. Ahluwalia, *Productivity and Growth in Indian Manufacturing*, 1991; A. K. Ghosh, *India's Defense Budget*, 1996; S. Gordon, "Indian Defense Spending: Treading Water in the Fiscal Deep," *Asian Survey*, 1992; Korea, *International Monetary Fund, International Financial Statistics Yearbook, 1998*; ACDA, *World Military Expenditures and Arms Transfers* (various issues); IISS, *The Military Balance* (various issues); Indonesia, same sources as for Korea, plus ILO, *Yearbook of Labor Statistics, 1997*, and *Economically Active Population Estimates and Populations, 1997*.

[a]Historical data on Japan's military investment share are not available. The 21 percent figure we used is derived from data shown in *Defense of Japan*, 1998, published by Japan's Defense Ministry.

[b]The 37.9 percent figure is not the rate of capital growth, but the investment rate (i.e., investment as a share of GDP), which as indicated has been quite stable in the reference decade. The 8–9 percent capital growth estimate reflects the authors' judgment in consideration of a plausible capital/output ratio of perhaps 4–5/1 for the economy as a whole.

[c]The figures shown, 10.12 percent for the mean, and 3.29 for the standard deviation (S.D.), refer to GDP growth rates, *not* productivity growth; the latter is estimated as a residual (about 1.5–2.0 percent annually in the prior decade) in the accounting model that we used. Assuming constancy of the other parameters in the model, a similarly relatively stable value of τ is inferred.

[d]Time series data on China's military investment share are not available. As indicated in the China section of Chapter Four, the relatively high investment share that we have assumed (25–32 percent) is based on the leadership's emphasis on military modernization, in part at the expense of force size.

[e]The extraordinarily wide range in capital growth for Korea results from several considerations: First, the International Monetary Fund investment data for Korea imply a decline in civilian capital in 1998 and 1999, net of depreciation; second, we assume that, over the forecast period, investment will gradually rise to a "long-run" growth rate of about 7 percent.

[f]The large difference in capital growth for Indonesia is mainly a result of the effect of the 1997 downturn. In gradually recovering from near-zero growth in 1998, Indonesia will likely show a capital stock gradual rise to a long-run rate of slightly above 7 percent.

preceding decade, although within one standard deviation thereof. The reasons for this judgment relate principally to what we have described in Chapter Four as the depth of Japan's structural economic problems, and the probable insufficiency of its reform efforts to bring about large and rapid remedies for these problems. A similar rationale applies to our judgment about the likely range of factor productivity (i.e., the parameter τ in Table B.1) in Japan during the forecast period.

For China, we have also made judgments that employment growth, capital growth, and productivity growth will be somewhat lower in the forecast period than in the prior decade. The rationale for these judgments relates largely to diminishing returns. The rationale for the assumed boost in military spending and military investment is summarized in Chapter Four and in footnote a of Table B.1.

For India, the reasons for judging that the key parameter values shown in Table B.1 will rise above their recent historical averages are discussed in Chapter Four. These reasons relate partly to more rapid economic growth achieved in the 1993–1997 period, and partly to the BJP's apparent success in gaining wider consensus for its goals of continued liberalization of the economy.

For Korea and Indonesia, both of which experienced several setbacks in the 1997–1998 economic turmoil, footnotes e and f of Table B.1 and Chapter Four provide the rationales for our assessment of the parameter values during the forecast period. These judgments are especially uncertain in Indonesia because of the serious political pressures threatening that country.

It is worth noting that, for all five countries, the parameters γ and π (see the right-side columns of Table B.1), which represent military spending shares in GDP and military investment shares in military spending, respectively, show remarkable stability (as reflected by the low standard deviations) in the previous decade. Consequently, the corresponding parameters used in our forecasts are close to the historical values, except for China, whose military spending share of GDP is raised for reasons described in Chapter Four.

Of course, despite their general pattern of stability, the military spending and investment parameters are inevitably subject to major uncertainties. For example, an apparently aggressive China might trigger sharp increases in these parameters in Japan; a significant retreat of Indonesia's military from the political domain might result in an appreciable reduction in military spending. However, the historic stability of military and investment spending parameters generally reflects strong organizational and bureaucratic influences, as well as inertia, and these forces are unlikely to change quickly.